"This eminently readable and relatable book illuminates the path to freedom for those on a quixotic quest for perfectionism. The authors guide the reader in understanding how perfectionism fails as a formula for living one's life, and endorse action consistent with values rather than feelings. So, if you or a loved one have perfectionism, or you provide care for those who do, this is without question a 'must-have' for your library."

—**Nancy Keuthen, PhD**, associate professor at Harvard Medical
School; and chief psychologist at the Center for OCD and
Related Disorders at Massachusetts General Hospital

"While perfectionism may promise you achievement and satisfaction, it instead leaves you strung out, unfulfilled, and never feeling 'good enough.' Built on a bedrock of what their research has shown to work, Clarissa Ong and Mike Twohig have written a warm, engaging, and practical guide to unwinding the binds of perfectionism. Follow in their footsteps to experience the freedom of living your life more flexibly and with greater compassion for imperfection."

—**Jennifer Kemp, MPsych**, clinical psychologist, and
author of *The ACT Workbook for Perfectionism*

"If you want to be more fully the person you *actually* want to be, not just the person your perfectionism says you *should* be, then this book will help. Using research-based strategies, it will help you become clearer on what you want your life to be about, overcome procrastination and rumination, and be kinder to yourself while also staying engaged and effective in life and relationships."

—**Jason Luoma, PhD**, CEO at Portland Psychotherapy,
shame and compassion researcher, and coauthor of
Learning ACT and *Values in Therapy*

T0000446

"Anxious perfectionism is a trap that can lead to surprising problems. Whether you are perfectionistic yourself, or have a perfectionist in your life, you don't want to miss this book! Clarissa Ong and Michael Twohig unpack perfectionism with relatable examples, humor, and deep understanding of its complexity. You'll learn how to be kinder toward yourself, get out of the anxiety-perfectionism cycle, and reconnect with what matters most in your life."

—**Debbie Sorensen, PhD**, coauthor of ACT *Daily Journal,*
and cohost of the *Psychologists Off the Clock* podcast

"Have you ever heard the saying, 'Don't let perfect be the enemy of good,' but struggled to find a way to put it into practice? Let this book be your (imperfect) guide. Clarissa Ong and Michael Twohig offer people suffering from maladaptive perfectionism an evidence-based model for letting go of the habits that tyrannize them, and giving themselves permission to be human."

—**Matthew S. Boone, LCSW**, peer-reviewed acceptance
and commitment therapy (ACT) trainer, and coauthor
of *Stop Avoiding Stuff*

"Carissa Ong and Michael Twohig have written a must-read book on overcoming the dark side of perfectionism: anxiety, worry, self-torture, and inaction. I am familiar with all of these states, and probably would have finished my education a year earlier if I had read this book. The authors take the reader on a journey that shows them what harmful perfectionism is, and how to overcome it and embrace the value of each moment."

—**Joseph Ciarrochi**, renowned scientist, author,
and coauthor of *What Makes You Stronger*

"Perfectionism is, at its core, an anxiety-based problem, in that perfectionists are anxious about coming up short, making mistakes, or even failing completely. Written by two internationally respected experts, *The Anxious Perfectionist* will teach you how to move past perfectionism though acceptance, mindfulness, self-compassion, and living life to the fullest. The book is filled with powerful methods for giving up the need for constant control and living a values-driven life based on what matters most to you. Everyone who struggles with perfectionism and anxiety should read this book!"

> —**Martin M. Antony, PhD, ABPP**, professor in the department of psychology at Ryerson University in Toronto, ON, Canada; and coauthor of *When Perfect Isn't Good Enough* and *The Anti-Anxiety Program*

"The old way was to tell people to 'stop and let go of those perfectionistic behaviors.' The new way is to acknowledge the challenge, difficulties, and struggles that come with perfectionism, and to compassionately teach skills that—one by one—lead a person to live a rich and peaceful life. In this book, Ong and Twohig, in a very real, compassionate, and skillful way, show their deep understanding of how the fear of messing things up, anxiety, search for perfection, urges to keep yourself busy, struggles with uncertainty, and not-good-enough stories interact with one another behind all perfectionistic behaviors. This is a perfect book for those prone to perfectionism! If you wonder how you can achieve more without losing yourself, then make sure to read this book! This book will help you to find your way in this imperfect, unpredictable, and uncertain life!"

> —**Patricia E. Zurita Ona, PsyD**, author of *Acceptance and Commitment Skills for Perfectionism and High-Achieving Behaviors* and *Living Beyond OCD Using Acceptance and Commitment Therapy*

The ANXIOUS PERFECTIONIST

HOW TO MANAGE PERFECTIONISM-DRIVEN ANXIETY
USING ACCEPTANCE & COMMITMENT THERAPY

CLARISSA W. ONG, PHD
MICHAEL P. TWOHIG, PHD

New Harbinger Publications, Inc.

Publisher's Note

Distributed in Canada by Raincoast Books

NEW HARBINGER PUBLICATIONS is a registered trademark of New Harbinger Publications, Inc.

New Harbinger Publications is an employee-owned company.

Copyright © 2022 by Clarissa W. Ong and Michael P. Twohig
New Harbinger Publications, Inc.
5720 Shattuck Avenue
Oakland, CA 94609
www.newharbinger.com

Cover design by Amy Shoup

Cover illustration by Sara Christian

Acquired by Elizabeth Hollis Hansen

Edited by Cindy Nixon

Library of Congress Cataloging-in-Publication Data

Names: Ong, Clarissa W., author. | Twohig, Michael P., author.
Title: The anxious perfectionist : how to manage perfectionism-driven anxiety using acceptance and commitment therapy / Clarissa W. Ong, Michael P. Twohig.
Description: Oakland, CA : New Harbinger Publications, [2022] | Includes bibliographical references.
Identifiers: LCCN 2021045014 | ISBN 9781684038459 (trade paperback)
Subjects: LCSH: Perfectionism (Personality trait) | Acceptance and commitment therapy. | Anxiety.
Classification: LCC BF698.35.P47 O65 2022 | DDC 155.2/32--dc23
LC record available at https://lccn.loc.gov/2021045014

Printed in the United States of America

25   24   23

10   9   8   7   6   5   4   3

This book is dedicated to our clients,
for finding the strength to be vulnerable.

Contents

Foreword

Over a century ago, Pierre Janet, a French psychologist and physician, saw in some of his patients a profound sense of incompleteness. This feeling tortured them, leading to intense doubts about the quality of not only their actions, but their perceptions as well. To cope with these doubts, they strove for perfection in both thought and deed. Their inability to achieve it led to even more intense efforts to avoid mistakes. The result was what Janet called *psychasthenia*, a combination of what we now consider a group of separate disorders consisting of obsessive-compulsive disorder, anxiety disorders, eating disorders, and mood disorders.

A few decades later, psychoanalyst Karen Horney saw something similar in her anxious patients who coped by trying to live up to idealized and perfectionistic images of themselves. These attempts were characterized by personal imperatives meant to guide behavior. Horney described these imperatives as the "tyranny of the should"—rigid dictates with which it was necessary to comply ("I should never make a mistake"; "I should never get less than an A"). Albert Ellis called such thinking "musterbation"—absolute and unrealistic demands for perfect performance. This book explores the "shoulds" and "musts" that characterize perfectionistic thinking and lead to emotional pain. If you see yourself in the descriptions of this type of thinking, you will come to understand just how harmful it is.

Pursuing perfection can lead to a fulfilling life, or it can lead you down a path of self-destruction. The difference is in how the pursuit is conducted. If mistakes and failures are accepted and used constructively, life can be expansive and affirming. If, on the other hand, mistakes and failures lead to attempts to avoid them, life becomes a struggle.

Perfectionism is inherently self-critical—an inflexible and extreme form of self-evaluation that results in feelings of failure and worthlessness, even in the face of considerable accomplishments. Regardless of how much you achieve, when your sense of self-worth depends on doing things perfectly and being perfect, the world becomes a constant source of threat with unending activities to fear and avoid. When people use mistakes or failures to determine their self-worth, the consequences are disastrous. Relentless self-criticism will lead you to believe there is something fundamentally wrong with you and only being perfect will make it okay.

Clarissa Ong and Michael Twohig explore how you can observe, understand, and accept your imperfections while at the same time strive to be your best. They explode the myth that self-criticism fuels success. As they point out, when self-criticism is the driving force for your performance, even if you experience some success, you will be miserable.

This book emphasizes the importance of values. Reading it will help you define the things that are truly important to you. It will assist you in clarifying and connecting with them. The mindfulness and compassion-based exercises will lead you closer to living the life you want. As with any such effort, the key will be to accept the inevitable mistakes and failures while striving to engage in what you most value in life. The journey will be well worth the effort.

—Randy O. Frost, PhD
Harold and Edna Siipola Israel Professor
Emeritus of Psychology
Smith College, Northampton, MA

The Anxiety, Stress, and Worry You Swim In

There are two sides to needing to do things perfectly. The bright side includes accolades after accolades, unmatched productivity, and consistent quality work. But there's a dark side: missed deadlines, intractable procrastination, quick irritability, and constant sleep deprivation. As therapists, we've worked with careerists who persist in the rat race even as their relationships fall apart, students who email professors with desperate deadline extension requests at 3:00 a.m., and retirees who look back on life and realize they weren't *really* there for most of it. As clinical psychologists, we've seen perfectionism leave some of our talented colleagues paralyzed and drained, sometimes even forced out of academia. This happens because perfectionism is a double-edged sword: the skills that help people be successful are the same ones that sabotage them in a fast-paced, high-pressure world. Anxiety, stress, and worry are the result.

This book was born of both professional and personal interest. My (Clarissa's) history has generously nurtured a need to be perfect, and I have watched perfectionism consume chunks of my life, promising that the ensuing success would be worth the losses. Although I've learned to be better at being imperfect, my fears and insecurities still linger. Every now and then, I allow perfectionism to decide my actions for me. In these moments, I'm struck by how difficult it is to ignore my desire for excellence.

Even coming up for a title for this book was a stressful back-and-forth. We had normal-ish options and a few that were more...niche. We were keenly aware of the irony of spending so much time and effort trying to come up with the "perfect" title even as we wrote about the illusion of perfection. So we did as we say. We picked a title that is "good enough," because letting go of perfectionism means we can live with messing up; it means we've given ourselves permission to be human. We have learned—and are still learning—to accept ourselves wholly, treat perfectionistic standards differently, and revel in the inescapable complexities of life. This is our wish for you.

We wrote this book for people who:

- Are mired in anxiety, stress, and worry over not being where they believe they *should* be

- Find that perfectionism has taken over their life

- Are interested in learning why they can't just let go of things

- Believe deep down that they're not good enough, unworthy, or unlovable

- Are done with perfectionism but don't quite know how to quit it

Reading this book and contemplating getting rid of your perfectionism may be scary. In fact, many of the people with whom we've worked find perfectionism to be a valuable part of who they are, and why wouldn't they? Perfectionism is absolutely helpful at times. That's why we want you to keep that part of you but learn new ways to interact with it.

You may procrastinate picking up this book until it is the "right" time or approach it like a manual or textbook, expecting to find in it the solution to your struggles. However, for this book to be most useful, we suggest reading it like you would watch a movie: just take it in. Take note of the parts that excite you. Gloss over the parts that are less relevant. Rewind if you've missed something important. Or read the whole thing once through and return to it later. Essentially, we want you to take what's helpful and leave the rest (most likely, you'll relate to certain examples much more than others). Read for fulfillment rather than for perfection. Then apply what you learn to your life.

At various points in this book, we'll be asking you to jot down your reactions and thoughts in the same place, like a section of your notebook, an online document, or a journal, so that you have something on which to reflect when you're done with the chapters. Our intention is for you to be able to save knowledge you've gleaned or any realizations you have and integrate them into your life instead of keeping them between the covers of this book. But ultimately, the choice is yours; this is not another "should."

We see perfectionism—and the anxiety, stress, and worry that come with it—similarly to the water surrounding schools of fish in the ocean: it's practically invisible, and you won't know what to do with it until you see it for what it is. That's because you can't respond—let alone respond effectively—to something you don't even know exists, even if not responding is hurting you. In the following pages, we try to make perfectionism—with its rules, standards, judgments, and more—transparent by describing how it works and the painful effects it has. We also provide skills you can use to navigate these waters more adeptly, based on our experiences working with perfectionism and knowledge about evidence-based treatments.

Our hope is that you'll gain insight into the full picture of your life and exercise your power to make choices in line with what matters to you. Living with perfectionism is not an either-or situation; you don't have to be beholden to it or completely cut it out of your life. There's another option: *befriend* perfectionism. Give it space to hang out when it gets annoying and enjoy it when it enriches your life. Find a middle path where you decide how much influence perfectionism has over your actions. This is a journey, and it may be more circuitous than you'd like. But at the end of the day, even if you've made one small change in a meaningful direction, that's progress.

CHAPTER 1

The Cost of Trying to Be the Best

Perfectionism has different functions. It can be about obtaining success, love, fame, prestige, recognition, wealth, praise, and so on. The logic goes, "If I am perfect, I will be successful" or some version of that statement. Something about your history or the current story you have about yourself says, "I won't be able to get what I want unless I am perfect."

Perfectionism can also be about preventing a mistake. In this case, you're less concerned about transforming the world; you just don't want to make any errors. You might believe, "If something goes wrong, it'll be my fault" or "I'll be judged for my mistakes." You might even worry you'd be letting people down by messing up.

Regardless of the function of your perfectionism, the actions you've taken and are taking to be perfect or to avoid being a failure take a toll in various ways. Though you may be aware of some of these negative effects, it's important to know exactly what the *total* cost of trying to be the best is. After all, you're the one paying it.

The Game of Perfectionism

Trying to either do things perfectly or avoid mistakes is a game. Moves you make in the game are associated with consequences; when your goals and actual outcomes match, you're playing the game "well." If you spent hours planning a camping trip to ensure things would go smoothly and the trip went swimmingly thanks to your planning, for example, your move worked. If the trip went terribly in spite of your planning, your move was ineffective. Winning the game means meeting your unrealistic goals, not making any mistakes, or finally feeling good about yourself and your accomplishments.

In order to win, you need to stay in the game, even as perfectionism lobs multiple fastballs your way: fear of failure, shame of being inadequate, stress over a messy home, worry about what others think of you, or the thought "I'm not good enough." What do you do with these thoughts and feelings? One option is to fight back: you work sixty-hour weeks, get a high-paying job, buy a McMansion, immaculately landscape your backyard, find the perfect partner(s), and scroll through endless online reviews to make sure you get the right espresso machine—all to show that you're *not* a failure, that you *are* enough. Winning means proving these thoughts and feelings wrong once and for all. And if you fall short in any way, you make up for it by working doubly hard next time. This is one way to win. Alas, there are side effects to using this "just be perfect" strategy:

- **Stress** manifests as muscle tension, headaches, irritability, and distorted appetite (skipping meals, overeating, and the like).

- **Worry** plagues your consciousness and rarely ever shuts up.

- **Anxiety** follows you throughout the day and to bed, keeping you awake at night.

So far, by remaining committed to this strategy, you've implicitly decided that the distress is worth the possibility of winning.

Alternatively, you may get so exhausted from playing against perfectionism that you lie down on the court and accept defeat: you choose the easier major in college, delay your application for a promotion, watch *Insecure* for the third time instead of unpacking bags, or procrastinate tasks until the day of the deadline. The idea is to not make any moves so that perfectionism can't fault you for anything or to make as few moves as possible, getting away with as little effort as you can. The strategy becomes "I can't fail if I don't try" or "Why bother if I can't be perfect?"

However, this is futile because giving up entrenches you in a rut of procrastination and guilt, so you lose either way.

The Price of Playing the Game

Think of perfectionism as a transaction: you pay a certain price to obtain a certain commodity. For instance, you pay three hours of sleep to get a higher grade on tomorrow's final. You give up watching a movie with your family to decrease the anxiety from letting your laundry sit out unfolded. You pay your emotional well-being for external approval. Throughout your life, you've been making these transactions at every decisional junction. Sometimes, you make these choices out of habit: "Of course I'm going to stay up late to make my slide deck impeccable; I'm not going to give a subpar presentation." Other times, the choices are deliberate: "It's fine to lose sleep and stress over all the details because I want this dinner party to go perfectly."

Unfortunately, the calculations in our head often belie reality. Losing sleep doesn't guarantee an A, just as sacrificing emotional health doesn't promise praise. You can overlook the dishonesty of these deals when you're constantly worried about moving on to the next task. Before you realize you didn't get the feeling of "good enough" in return for years of hard work in graduate school, you're already stressing over preparing a job application for the next phase of your career. As soon as you return from your family road trip, you start worrying about planning your next vacation.

Moreover, there are usually hidden costs that don't factor into your decision making. Less sleep may also impact your mood and make you less desirable to be around, compromising the quality of your interpersonal interactions. Being overly focused on event planning may lead to frustration from others who just want you to be a part of the celebration and cost you invitations to future parties. Your emotional health may suffer not only in the short term, but also for months (and years) afterward. All these considerations go into the price of playing the game.

Take a moment to reflect on what playing the game of perfectionism has been like for you. In your notebook, answer the questions below. Take your time. Don't let your brain answer the questions. Through living your life, you've been collecting data on your in-game performance, kind of like your own sabermetrics (as in *Moneyball*), so listen to the wisdom of your lived experience.

1. **What have you given up to stay in the game?** This is the cost of engaging with perfectionism. Include the time, energy, sleep, relationships, self-respect, dreams, and freedoms you have relinquished to focus your efforts on being perfect. Track the physical and emotional toll of the anxiety, stress, and worry that come with needing things to go or be a certain way. How many precious present moments have you lost to the nonstop prattle in your head? How do the anxiety-induced sleepless nights leave you feeling the next day? How much have you compromised your values to please others? What is it like for you when loved ones say they feel neglected or frustrated due to your unwillingness to compromise? What physical symptoms show up when you jeopardize your mental and emotional well-being to strive for perfection?

2. **What are you getting out of playing the game?** This is the reward associated with trying to be perfect or avoiding mistakes. Perhaps people think you're smart, you excel in everything you do, or you successfully distract yourself from thoughts about being an utter failure. Playing the game has benefits; you wouldn't have stayed in the game for as long as you have if you didn't gain anything from it. Consider what those benefits are.

3. **What have you done to try to beat perfectionism?** Reflect on the strategies—helpful and unhelpful—you've used to solve, fix,

overcome, or deal with perfectionism. Be comprehensive and specific; for example, appealing to your willpower, telling yourself that you're a failure to increase motivation, quadruple-checking your work, avoiding tasks that seem too difficult, procrastinating important tasks until the last minute, taking on more projects than is reasonable, always saying yes to other people, visiting a dozen stores to find the perfect tomato seedlings, spending hours preparing your grocery list, or pretending everything is fine even when it feels like your world is collapsing in on itself. List at least five strategies you've tried in your notebook.

4. **How effective have these strategies (from the previous question) been at helping you beat perfectionism?** Evaluate their short-term and long-term effectiveness (create a column for each), that is, winning a set versus winning the match. Be honest with yourself. How much closer are you to winning the game and being done with this incessant volley for good? Winning means believing you are enough and never having to deal with the anxiety, stress, and worry of perfectionism ever again.

Once you've answered these four questions, reflect on whether fighting with perfectionism or pursuing perfection has been a wise investment *for you*. The only standard that matters here is you and your well-being. Don't just take into account the cost (question 1); also factor in what you're getting out of the game (question 2). Weigh your answer to question 1 against that to question 2. Has the overall cost of perfectionism been worth the reward? Jot down your reactions to this question. There is no right or wrong reaction; give yourself space to face the full implications of playing against perfectionism for so long.

Next, look at your answer to question 4 and write down any reactions you have to your evaluation of the effectiveness of your strategies.

Again, resist responding too quickly. Sit with any realizations (or nonrealizations) you're having—any and all experiences are allowed here.

People usually find that their strategies are effective in the short term but amplify stress in the long term. As a result, they conclude that they need better long-term strategies. This analysis makes sense. In fact, it's what any decent athlete would advise. But what if *this* game is not about your intelligence, strength, or perseverance? Surely, if perfectionism were a solvable problem, you would have figured it out by now (check out your list of strategies in question 3). We suspect you're highly motivated to fix perfectionism (whatever that means for you) and have spent a great deal of time and energy on this endeavor. Your lack of talent or effort is not the issue here. Instead, what if this is an unwinnable game to begin with? Listen to your life data on this.

Now take this exercise a step further, beyond effectiveness: Are your strategies making you love your life, feel the way you hoped you would, or be a better person to be around? Answer a few more questions in your notebook:

- Are you more satisfied with your life now than you were a year ago?

- Is life going the way you want it to go?

- Is a life dominated by anxiety, stress, and worry a worthy pursuit?

- What's going to happen if you keep letting this game rule your life?

Take your time to contemplate these questions. They're important for setting the stage for why you're working on perfectionism. To be clear, this isn't fearmongering; if playing the game of perfectionism makes you content, absolutely keep doing what you're doing. But if not, we want you to be honest with yourself about whether you like your life *as it is*. Are you truly happy in the profoundest sense of the word? We don't mean, "Are you laughing and smiling all the time?" We mean, "Does your heart feel full and your soul feel nourished even when you have long days and encounter tough situations?" If you believe you'll eventually enjoy life at some point in the future, how much longer are you willing to wait and how long have you already been waiting?

Based on stories from people with whom we've worked, we know that staying in the game can lead to some version of falling so behind on tasks that you give up entirely, looking back on your life and realizing you were miserable for most of it, missing out on life as it is happening because you need to optimize and plan all the time, feeling significantly more burnt out than your peers, choosing to do things that are easier or more manageable but less meaningful, or even sabotaging constructive relationships when others do not meet your standards. You know this. Your struggle is bigger than perfectionism; you probably care about much more in your life than being successful or not messing up. Remember that there is a lot waiting for you off the court. So why do you continue to pour your resources into this game? With a clearer sense of the costs, benefits, and effectiveness of perfectionism, let's examine the origins of the need to be perfect.

The Roots of Perfectionism

Why is it so difficult to be wrong, sit with uncertainty, or let go of the need to do things a particular way even when you know everyone is getting annoyed with you? You probably didn't choose to feel constantly stressed over your inability to meet impossible standards or to douse yourself with self-criticism whenever you make the slightest mistake. Where did perfectionism come from, and when did it start taking over your life?

Perfectionism has roots in your personal history. Perhaps you grew up around adults with high expectations who doled out approval only when you met those expectations. For example, you got praise from your parents only when you did well in school or made friends they liked.

Therefore, early on, you learned that the only way to acquire affection was to excel or to fit the mold set out for you; doing what you cared about didn't get you what every human fundamentally needs: social acceptance. Conversely, minor mistakes were emphasized and criticized, so you became extra cautious. You learned that being perfect or never making mistakes makes you lovable; as an intelligent being, you probably also deduced that being who you are makes you *unlovable*.

Perhaps your caregivers wanted you to succeed at all costs because they believed doing better and pushing yourself harder would put you in a position to have a happy life. As a result, every time you achieved, they wanted more. After you won a part in the school play, they asked why you didn't get the lead role. After your first violin recital, they reminded you to stay on tempo. After you learned the forehand with much difficulty, they told you to start learning the backhand. If this is the message you heard countless times throughout childhood and adolescence—that you "can" and "should" do more—then, by now, you probably feel like, at your core, you aren't good enough. How could you not? The only way to be good enough is to be perfect. If you're perfect, then you can't be better and you can finally stop doing more.

Or perhaps you were perfect. You won races, got straight A's, and aced all the school performances. You got used to being perfect and all the concomitant rewards: praise, popularity, pride. Then you reached a point where perfection became harder to attain; your classmates got smarter, work got more complicated, and life asked more of you than it ever had. You realized you were not as talented as you had believed (or been told), that even if you tried as hard as you did before, you still wouldn't be the best. In that case, what's the point? It's perfection or nothing, and it's more mortifying to fail trying than to fail not trying, so somewhere along the way, you decided to take the safer route and stop trying.

Everyone has their own story of how perfectionism took root and crept into the crevices of their lives. You might have a completely different narrative from the ones we described. Still, there was likely some component wherein being perfect was encouraged or rewarded and being less than perfect was frowned upon or even punished. Those are the core ingredients for a perfectionistic view of the world. Reflect on your unique history. What are the roots of your need to be perfect? How do you see them threading through your life today? Write your perfectionism narrative down in your notebook.

The Pressure to Chase the Unattainable

Perfection exists figuratively, not literally. Trying to be perfect may be reasonable if perfection is attainable, but it's not. The whole point of perfection is that *nothing* is good enough; there's always a flaw, a mistake, a misstep in real life. Furthermore, the definition of perfection constantly changes; what was perfect when you first started a task is no longer perfect when you get there. Hence, pursuing perfection is akin to chasing a nonexistent entity—you'll never catch it no matter how fast you run. It's kind of like playing a game in which your opponent keeps altering the rules whenever you get ahead: it's unfair and exhausting.

The capriciousness of perfectionism plays out in painful ways. Recall a lofty goal you achieved at some point in your life, something you had initially thought you would be unlikely to achieve because it was accessible to only the most special, the brightest, or the strongest. It could have been a scholarship, a job, a certain number of friends, or a personal pull-up record. You worked assiduously toward this goal, believing that accomplishing it would give you the validation you craved. You might even have had it in your mind that achieving this goal would unequivocally prove that you were worthy.

What happened when you reached this goal? Did you win the game like you were supposed to, or did the rules change? Did you say, "Yes, I did it and I'm amazing," or did you immediately dismiss the accomplishment as "not a big deal" and start nitpicking your faults? The reality is that perfection is an illusion for which you've been conditioned to strive, so you keep getting tricked into playing an unwinnable game.

What Do You Want?

There are things that matter outside of winning the game. You know this intuitively if you've ever felt conflicted between doing what you know society, peers, or authority figures want you to do and doing what you want to do. For instance, you signed up for piano lessons instead of playing with your friends after school. You took biology instead of art history. You volunteered to bake cupcakes for a church event—again. You accepted a job with the big-name company instead of the one that prioritizes employee welfare. You stayed married to avoid being divorced at thirty.

The result of always trying to please others is that you don't know what you care about independent of external input, because you've never considered your own needs and wants. After all, identifying and stating *your* needs and wants didn't gain you approval; in fact, the opposite action of identifying *others'* expectations of you and living up to them made you more acceptable. Take this in: you've been trained to prioritize others' needs at the expense of your own, and you've been practicing this for years—to the point that it's basically automatic. So *of course* you're going to watch your friend's fish even if it means bailing on your weekend plans. *Of course* you're going to invite fifty people you haven't seen in ten years to your wedding. You readily relegate your own needs as a matter of habit, and to the extent that these decisions are unconscious, you may not realize that trying to get others to like and accept you is the reason you do what you do.

As a thought experiment, see if you can let go of all the imposed standards, wants, and expectations. Pretend you're already perfect and have nothing left to prove. If you had no one to answer to but yourself, what would you want out of your time on this planet? It could be developing deep connections with people, making a positive impact on the environment, exploring all this world has to offer—its cliffs, oceans, cities, and cultures—or nurturing a new life, watching your child toddle, fall, and get back up again. In your notebook, write down whatever comes to mind.

As you consider what you want for yourself, visualize a scene that fills you with joy and warmth, and then answer the following questions:

- Where are you?

- Who is around you?

- What are you doing?

- What are you feeling?

- What do you see and hear?

- Finally, how much does this scene overlap with your current pursuit of perfection?

Joy, warmth, and perfectionism don't quite go together. In fact, trying to be perfect leads to ongoing anxiety, stress, and worry. In trying to eradicate errors, be ultracompetent, and be liked, you've given up valuable time and energy. The problem with this trade-off is that the time and energy you've spent haven't actually made you more perfect or content, mainly because perfection is a false idol. However, these consequences aren't immediately obvious, so you keep trying to beat perfectionism. In fact, your upbringing and societal norms pressure you to keep playing the game of perfectionism.

You might even have convinced yourself that trying to win is exactly what you want, so you find yourself stuck in a rigged game, believing your only options are to keep trying to win or to accept defeat. We disagree, and most of this book explains why—and what we see as an alternative. But before we get to what to do with perfectionism, it's helpful to first look the beast straight in the eye and confront what you've been fighting (and losing to) all this time.

CHAPTER 2

When Perfectionism Gets in Your Way

As long as you're playing the game of perfectionism, you're losing. You're losing opportunities to be present with loved ones, to embark on adventures that carry inherent uncertainty, and to discover your full potential beyond the confines of perfectionism. The lens of perfectionism colors everything you see, which makes it difficult to conceive of a space free from its influence and rid of the constant reminders to "do more" and "not mess up." This is why it's critical to get a good look at the very lens through which you've been experiencing the world. Once you can see a version of your life without perfectionism, you'll have a clearer sense of how to proceed. Thus, before getting to skills and strategies, the first thing to do is to understand how perfectionism works and recognize it when it shows up in your life.

Clarifying Perfectionism

Perfectionism is broadly defined as working toward high standards and expectations. The "overachiever" is the prototype most people think of when we talk about perfectionism. However, perfectionism is more nuanced than overachieving; it shows up in multiple ways: the neighbor whose fence remains unpainted because they can't decide between eggshell or ivory white, the friend who has a meltdown unless things go exactly according to plan, the artist who has produced nothing despite spending hours in the studio, or the graduate student who spends more time organizing tasks than doing them. All these people could be perfectionists.

There are two types of perfectionism: *adaptive* and *maladaptive* (Bieling, Israeli, and Antony 2004; Stoeber and Damian 2014). Adaptive perfectionism describes a pattern of striving for achievement that is perceived as rewarding or meaningful; it is associated with positive outcomes like self-reported happiness, life satisfaction, and conscientiousness (Stoeber and Otto 2006; Suh, Gnilka, and Rice 2017). Adaptive perfectionists can function at high levels of productivity without burning themselves out. They like this style of living, and it works for them.

In contrast, maladaptive perfectionism is characterized by self-criticism, rigid pursuit of unrealistically high standards, distress when standards are not met, and dissatisfaction even when standards are met. Unsurprisingly, maladaptive perfectionism is linked to such psychological conditions as depression, obsessive-compulsive disorder, eating disorders, and anxiety disorders (Egan, Wade, and Shafran 2011). It is also correlated with more subsequent daily stress and negative mood (Prud'homme et al. 2017). These associations appear to be consistent across cultures (Park and Jeong 2015), which means maladaptive perfectionism is likely cross-culturally relevant. Maladaptive perfectionism undermines precisely what it is intended to achieve—be it success, happiness, or productivity.

You may recognize some of this in yourself. If so, you hardly enjoy what you do. The doing is stressful because you berate yourself the whole time, and being done with a task is disappointing because no outcome is ever good enough. Alternatively, you may be so overwhelmed by your high standards that taking any step forward seems daunting; you don't want to fail by making the wrong move, so you don't move at all. An outsider might see this as being unmotivated or lazy when, in fact, you're desperately spinning your wheels with nothing to show for it. This is how maladaptive perfectionism gets in the way.

There are three salient distinctions between adaptive and maladaptive perfectionism.

Approach versus avoidance. Adaptive and maladaptive perfectionism are differentiated by the *reason behind*—or *function of*—the perfectionistic behavior. That is, what is the motivation for striving? In adaptive perfectionism, the motivation is typically to *approach* a desired consequence (positive reinforcement), whereas in maladaptive perfectionism, the motivation is to *avoid* or *escape* an undesirable consequence (negative reinforcement; Bieling, Israeli, and Antony 2004). Positive reinforcement is the proverbial carrot and negative reinforcement the stick.

Basically, do you act to obtain a reward or to avoid an aversive consequence? For example, always completing your work on time could be adaptive or maladaptive. If completing work is about deriving a sense of satisfaction from meaningful engagement with the work, then it's adaptive. But if completing work is about avoiding negative evaluation from your supervisor, it's maladaptive. If you've been debating for hours whether to pick the flight that lands at 1:00 or 3:30 p.m. because you aren't sure of the optimal time to circumvent traffic, that's maladaptive because you're trying to *avoid* the aversive state of being wrong. Undesirable consequences can be real-world events like failing a job interview or inner experiences like feeling inadequate. Generally, adaptive perfectionism is about seeking achievement that is experienced as fulfilling, whereas maladaptive perfectionism is about avoiding failure.

Process versus outcome. Perfectionism can be process- or outcome-oriented. Process-oriented perfectionism overlaps with adaptive perfectionism; it's about savoring the process of tasks and finding meaning in doing them regardless of outcome. This is the aspiring baker who continues to bake even after producing pastries with soggy bottoms and dry genoise sponge cakes. Outcome-oriented perfectionism cares only about results, such that an imperfect result negates all effort.

The distinction between process and outcome matters because you have more control over your actions and how you do them (process) than the results of your actions (outcome). If you make outcome your metric of success, then success falls outside your control; but if you define success based on process or how you approach tasks, then you can control how successful you are. For example, which do you have more control over: learning new things *with curiosity* or getting an A on every test? *Being present* during your child's first birthday party or making sure everyone has fun? Showing up as a *genuine* person or getting people to like you?

The problem with focusing on outcome is that you feel like you're continuously grasping for something that's just outside your reach, living in a limbo of "almost." The dinner party was *almost* perfect, except you burned the green beans. Your week was *almost* perfect, except you missed yoga Tuesday morning. The proximity to perfection is probably what's so dangerous because it deludes you into believing that the outcome you want is within reach—so you keep trying...and trying. In contrast, if you focus on process, you might find some pleasure in simply doing things and letting go of expectations to be better. In the "process" space, you can be exactly as you are.

Casual versus committed. Adaptive and maladaptive perfectionists also interact with their standards differently. If you're nice to yourself when you fall short of your ambitions, you're likely on the adaptive end. In a sense, you have a casual relationship with your high standards. You appreciate them if they're adding something positive to your life and ignore them if they're not; you're not obligated to do anything for them. The adaptive perfectionist may also be more realistic about their capabilities relative to their standards and accepting of their own limitations. Thus, they can aim high, miss the mark, and still be satisfied with their effort. In other words, adaptive perfectionists are more likely to give themselves a break when they mess up.

In contrast, if you're unyielding with your standards and measure your self-worth in terms of your ability to meet these standards, you're probably on the maladaptive end. In this case, you're in a committed relationship with your high standards; you're heavily invested in and hyperresponsive to them. In addition, you experience distress when you fail to meet their demands and find yourself doing everything you can to placate them. For maladaptive perfectionists, failure is unbearable and triggers intense shame and guilt. This is a grim existence.

A Deeper Look at Maladaptive Perfectionism

Predictably, this book focuses on maladaptive perfectionism, so we'll explain it in more detail. The first thing to know is that ruthless self-criticism lies at the core of maladaptive perfectionism. When we say "ruthless self-criticism," we mean things you'd never say to anyone (besides yourself):

- "You'll never be good enough."

- "No one will ever accept you for who you are."

- "You are and will always be a failure."

- "You're broken and nothing you do will change that."

Self-criticism plays like an infinitely repeating AI playlist that learns your deepest insecurities and only becomes more caustic over time. It selectively gathers evidence—throwing out any contradictory claims of your adequacy—and torments you with the "reality" of your worthlessness. Self-criticism may not be an issue if we treat it lightly, as if a five-year-old were heckling us. However, it leads to tremendous emotional stress when taken as truth (more on this in chapter 5).

A second feature of maladaptive perfectionism is rigid adherence to rules, expectations, and standards, such as:

- You *have to* always do the right thing.

- Don't turn in work *unless* it's flawless.

- Making a mistake *means* you're a loser.

- Only act *if you're sure* you're making the correct decision.

- You *must* be successful in everything you do.

Rigid adherence means rules must be followed and standards must be met at all costs, even if you're sacrificing meals, sleep, family time, dating, exercise, and hobbies. Any deviation from rules and expectations proves you're incompetent, stupid, pathetic, naïve, and so forth, so you work zealously to meet one expectation after another.

The problem with needing to adhere to rules and standards is that you can't win—in fact, you can only lose. Standards and expectations are set excessively high, and the margin of error is obscenely small. The odds are tremendously stacked against you, leaving you trapped in an unfair uphill battle.

The third piece of maladaptive perfectionism is that its standards are subjective, making it tricky to determine whether you meet them, because you can always argue for either direction ad infinitum. More often, you'll use the subjectivity to convince yourself that you've failed, like when meeting a deadline isn't good enough because you could've gotten it done sooner or when positive evaluations don't indicate success because people are just being nice. Perfectionism makes it so that even if you meet a predetermined standard, it doesn't count, because if you managed to accomplish the goal, it was too easy to begin with.

If you've ever struggled to complete a task "successfully," recall how you operationalized success. Did you have an objective rubric that concretely described the criteria for completion, or was "success" based on an arbitrary benchmark that required you to feel good about the task? When you're up against slippery definitions and perpetually changing rules, your best will never be enough.

Examples of Perfectionistic Behaviors

Perfectionism is defined by what it is intended to achieve or its purpose (that is, its function). Hence, a specific set of behaviors cannot encompass all of perfectionism. Any action can be perfectionistic if it's about trying to prove abilities, trying to avoid making mistakes, following a rule about how to be successful, or attempting to meet an unreasonable expectation. The person who is high-achieving in several domains, pays excessive attention to details, is absurdly organized, and is maximally efficient is one type of perfectionist. The person who turns in excellent work right at the deadline but skipped grocery shopping, going to the gym, and their sister's birthday party to make it happen is another type of perfectionist. So is the person who is always late, has a messy living space, procrastinates everything, and is perpetually distracted. Although these presentations look different, they serve the same perfectionistic function.

Conversely, behaviors that look similar can have different functions. For example, procrastination could be about (a) being more interested in leveling up in World of Warcraft than vacuuming (not perfectionism) or (b) indecisiveness due to a perceived need to make the "right" choice (perfectionism). In the latter case, the rule is that you can't commit to a decision until you're certain that the decision is correct. But because humans live in perpetual uncertainty, you never make any decision.

Another rule underlying perfectionistic procrastination is that you can't proceed with a task until you know how to do it correctly. Again, because you can't know for sure how to do something perfectly before you do it, you remain stuck, at a loss for what to do next. These situations can feel overwhelming as you simultaneously experience immense pressure to do things "right" and utter confusion over how to do that. Given these cognitive and emotional roadblocks, in the absence of a deadline, people can procrastinate a project literally for years, whether it's wallpapering the basement, fixing the broken bike in the garage, or finding a primary care provider in a new city.

Perfectionism takes so many forms that it's actually easier to define it in terms of its function. As you get adept at recognizing the reason behind or function of your behaviors, you'll know when and how to change behaviors to improve your well-being. The change we want for you is not necessarily *what* you're doing—it's *why* you're doing what you're doing. At the end of this book, your life might even look the same to an unknowing observer. However, we hope that you'll be organizing your folder tabs, alphabetizing your book collection, and working during your vacation because you find purpose in those activities, not because a rule says you *should*.

✽ ✽ ✽

In this chapter, we've described two types of perfectionism: adaptive and maladaptive. Adaptive perfectionism is experienced as rewarding and meaningful—this is the kind of perfectionism most of us envy; it creates overachievers who somehow have fun being brilliant. In contrast, maladaptive perfectionism is experienced as punitive and unsustainable—it feeds self-criticism, self-doubt, anxiety, stress, worry, guilt, shame, and depression. It besieges us with unattainable expectations and, ultimately, leads to burnout or avoidance and procrastination. Maladaptive perfectionism is a catch-22: you can try hard and still feel like a failure because your standards are too high or constantly adjusted, or you can give up and automatically become a failure.

The distress, avoidance, and futile striving associated with maladaptive perfectionism is what we're targeting and aiming to change with this book. In the chapters that follow, we lay out skills to help you navigate the maelstrom of perfectionism and retake control over your life. We start with the skill of acknowledging the cacophony of perfectionism without letting it boss you around.

CHAPTER 3

Acknowledging the Noise Without Surrendering to It

Perfectionism is exhausting. We know this from listening to our clients describe all their stresses, anxieties, fears, worries, what-ifs, and worst-case scenarios. Sometimes, we get caught up in their worries even when the whole point of our work is to help them let go of them. Because what if our client dies alone with seventeen cats feasting on their undiscovered, decomposing corpse? "You definitely *have to* problem solve that," says perfectionism. This rhetoric is probably familiar to you. Sure, let go of those *other* unimportant worries, but not *this* one. This one has real consequences; you *need* to hold on to this one. When you find yourself backed into a corner, when it feels like you're trying to keep uncountable plates spinning as the world keeps adding more and more, when you're scripting multiple scenarios to plan for all the possible contingencies, you might be at the mercy of perfectionism.

Why "Stop Worrying" Is Bad Advice

On some level, it would be easier to not care or worry about anything. That way, you wouldn't have to spend your mental and emotional energy dealing with the (admittedly unlikely) scenarios of becoming food for your ungrateful pets, never getting the job you want, never attaining success, never being loved, or making an irreversible mistake. But you can't just stop worrying because you decide to or because someone tells you to. Otherwise, you'd have done that years ago. The solution isn't to "stop worrying," because that's unworkable.

Asking someone to "stop worrying" is fundamentally different from asking them to "stop taking thirty-minute showers." In reality, it's closer to "stop making it rain." Worry is not entirely within your control, so you can't make it do anything. In fact, thoughts are automatic a lot of the time; they show up and leave at whim. Yes, you can conjure positive affirmations and you can try to create a grocery list right as you're falling asleep, but these probably aren't the thoughts you're hoping to change.

We're referring to thoughts—like "I'm broken" and "I'll never be enough"—that can't be swept away no matter how much you argue with them and regardless of how much praise you receive. For example, you may struggle to choose a destination for your upcoming vacation because you don't know that you're making the "right" choice—even after all the hours spent perusing travel blogs, reading dozens of Wikipedia pages, and debating with your partner. These stickier thoughts do as they please; trying to get rid of them (like the objects in your home that no longer spark joy) not only is ineffective, but probably even serves to strengthen them. Nevertheless, you continue to try.

The reason you respond like this is that you take your thoughts seriously. Of course you do. Listening to the sounds in your head generally keeps you alive and healthy. "Stop on a red light." "Don't go near the edge of the cliff." "Eat more vegetables." The problem with taking thoughts seriously *all the time* is that they're sometimes unhelpful. Moreover, you may miss when they're unhelpful because you're so used to automatically structuring your life in terms of thoughts, especially rules and scripts. For example, you don't relearn restaurant etiquette every time you go out to eat; you follow your restaurant script. You may encounter the unique restaurant that encourages you to be condescending to staff and tip poorly, but it's much more efficient to use a heuristic and be wrong 0.1 percent of the time than to laboriously analyze every new situation on the off chance that your heuristic is wrong. As much as it's in your interest to listen to your thoughts most of the time, they can also be used against you by perfectionism.

Rules and Reasons in Perfectionism

The most effective weapon perfectionism has is rules. Rules are the metaphorical metal bars that keep you from talking to new people, being vulnerable with romantic partners, being flexible when things go wrong, starting (or finishing) a craft project, and cutting yourself slack when you need it the most. Not only do these rules stop you from doing things you care about, but they simultaneously push you to do things that decrease your well-being, like skipping meals, overworking, compromising personal boundaries, and missing family gatherings. You don't even have to see the bars for them to affect you; in fact, they probably work better *because* you don't know they're there. If you can see the bars, you might be able to figure out how to navigate around them, but it's harder to deal with a barrier you don't even know exists.

Without rules, perfectionism is powerless. More precisely, without *your obedience* to rules, perfectionism is powerless. Can you remember the first time you broke a rule (no matter how small) and nothing happened? Think about arbitrary rules you never questioned, like having to wake up at a certain time, put away your clothes in a certain way, or wait two hours after eating before going swimming.

When you broke the rule, you might have been stressed about the consequences you'd have to face. Then, nothing happened. No one cared. In that moment, you realized that you'd been taking the rule much more seriously than was warranted, and certainly much more seriously than anyone around you. That is, rules didn't matter as much as you believed they did—or as much as perfectionism convinced you they did. For example, as a teen, I, Mike, and some of my friends set off fireworks outside the dates that were allowed. The police showed up, lectured us, and drove each of us home. The police told my mom what I did, and she sent me to my room. I was fearful of what my dad would do when he got home, but when I saw him the next morning, he only said, "Hey, Sparky, I heard you got a ride from the cops." That experience undermined my rule about how unreasonable my parents would be if I got into trouble. It's the same with most other rules. You just haven't learned yet that they're much bigger in your head than in real life.

One way perfectionism keeps those bars invisible, so that you continue to be constrained by them unknowingly, is by hiding the source of rules. When rules are really about fear of failure and disappointing others, perfectionism lets you think that they're about helping you get what *you* want. Consider the rule "I must be liked." Is this because you truly care about connecting with others, or are you trying to avoid social rejection? If you're unsure, it's probably the latter. You don't hesitate when someone asks you if you truly care about your grandparents, your dog, your integrity, or your health, because there's something about these things that matter to you on a deeper—almost primal—level. The issue with being unclear about the source of rules is that you therefore don't know if they're worth following. If rules were about you and your needs— for example, ride a bike with a helmet on—you'd probably want to follow them even if you didn't feel like it. But in the case of perfectionistic rules, they're about fear. They're about protecting you from threats you have yet to—or may never—encounter *at the cost of* your wants and needs.

Another technique perfectionism uses to make you unquestioningly follow rules is providing reasons for the rules. These reasons only need to sound like reasons; they don't even need to be legitimate to influence your behavior. For example, you might follow a rule like, "Everything I produce must be excellent *because* that's the kind of person I am." This is the pattern: *rule* because *reason*. If you strictly adhere to the rule of excellence, believing it to be sensible, even a routine email to your boss needs to be done well. Thus, you proofread it a couple of times. You ask your coworkers for feedback. You proofread it several more times. In reality, the situation doesn't call for this level of conscientiousness because your boss isn't going to spend more than five seconds skimming the email. It's just an email, but the rules say you must do it right, and the rules are justified by reasons. Meanwhile, what does "that's the kind of person I am" even mean?

Fortifying rules with reasons works because humans like coherence. We like having reasons for our actions, we like engaging in actions based on reasons, and we generally like stories with as few contradictions as possible. Whenever you try to fill gaps in a story ("That makes sense because…"), come up with reasons for your actions ("I'm doing this because…"), or explain why the rules you follow are reasonable ("I can't make mistakes because…"), you're playing Perfectionism Says—like the children's game Simon Says, but with perfectionism giving the orders. In Perfectionism Says, everything must make sense and everything that makes sense must be taken seriously.

As you register the extent to which perfectionistic rules sculpt your life, you may wonder where the rules are coming from. This is more *coherence seeking* (needing an explanation for events and observations). That's how your mind works. But the answer to exactly where rules and reasons emanate from is unclear; we can't trace a rule to a specific event in your childhood. That's because our brains are infinitely complex, and the origin of any particular thought is practically unknowable. The closest we can get is to acknowledge that thoughts are a product of our developmental history, our broader environment (interpersonal networks, social mores, and such), and our current context (like if you're watching TV, feeling hungry, or just had a fight with your best friend). Together, these factors create cognitive chaos that our desire for coherence demands we either (1) simplify by ignoring contradictory pieces of the picture or (2) effectively parse by spinning a cogent narrative around the disparate pieces. However, neither of those options is feasible, because (1) we can't just pretend our experiences didn't happen, and (2) our thoughts are random and so necessarily fail to fit neat story lines.

Review all the thoughts you've had in the past few minutes: concepts in this book (we hope), your to-do list, your next appointment, what to eat next, what you ate last, the new show all your coworkers are talking about, what your friend meant when they said your haircut looked good but avoided eye contact... You get the point. The world isn't simple enough to be condensed into a linear narrative, and, in fact, it doesn't make sense a lot of the time—it's not supposed to. It doesn't make sense that you can feel angry and loving toward someone. It doesn't make sense that you can feel hungry and not want to eat. It doesn't make sense that you can like and hate yourself. Yet these contradictory experiences can all be true. Even if perfectionism insists otherwise, your experiences tell you indisputably that coherence is specious. To subvert perfectionism, you need to expose its coherence propaganda.

Expose the Game

When you don't see the rules governing your behavior, you may perceive your rule following as freely chosen actions—and if your actions are freely chosen, why change them? So recognize whenever you're playing Perfectionism Says. Only by checking yourself in this way do you have the chance to opt out. One way to identify rules and expose the game's mechanics is to familiarize yourself with the common sentence structures in which perfectionistic thoughts are embedded. They include:

- **I should** (meet all my deadlines).

- **I should not** (still be mad over that comment).

- **I have to** (get rid of my anxiety).

- **I must** (make the right decision).

- **I need to** (feel motivated) **before** (I make a change in my life).

- **If I** (feel sad when friends don't reply to my texts), **it means I** (am pathetic).

- **I can't** (switch jobs at this point in my career).

- **I'm too** (needy) **to** (be in a relationship).

You'll also need to catch reasons, which are easier to identify; they typically appear after the word "because."

- **Because...**I need to prove myself to others.

- **Because...**I don't want people to think I'm dumb.

- **Because...**I care about being successful.

- **Because...**I want my parents to be proud of me.

- **Because...**I'm better than this.

Reasons are particularly dangerous when they're used to rationalize unhelpful behaviors in the name of coherence. For example, it might make sense to stay up until 2:30 a.m. to realign tables in your slide deck *because* you care about professionalism. *Action* because *reason* = coherent story. The semblance of an explanation shields reasons from scrutiny, so you go along with them. But practice being skeptical this time and inspect the reason.

1. How do perfectly aligned tables demonstrate professionalism?

2. Are there more effective ways to demonstrate professionalism?

3. Is the trade-off of sleep for aligned tables *really* about professionalism?

If you take a closer look, you'll see that some reasons quickly fall apart. It seems that our minds care more about a *feeling* of coherence than *actual* coherence with what's going on in the world. For instance, you might convince yourself that you're not as frustrated with your roommate as you really are *because* you're not petty. If you're not petty, you wouldn't feel frustrated over something as trivial as them leaving the lights on overnight. That's the coherent version, so you believe it, even as you resentfully turn off the lights the next morning. Or you might have a story about how you're not "fit" enough to run marathons, so you cap your running limit at five miles. That makes sense; you're not an athletic person, so that's not something you do, and your marathon dream evaporates on cue. Attachment to coherence makes it so that you frequently settle for an ostensibly coherent story at the expense of honoring your actual experiences or moving toward your goals.

Coherence has a cost. Ask yourself if you're willing to pay it. If not, what can you do instead?

The Limitations of Logic

Exposing the game of Perfectionism Says can create a vacuum in your life depending on how much your actions have been shaped by rules and reasons. All of a sudden, you've lost a guiding force. If you stop doing things "because you want to be successful" or "because you don't want to mess up," then how will you decide what to do next? Recognizing that rules and reasons are part of a game we didn't know we were playing shatters the illusion of coherence; it dismantles the stories we've been telling ourselves (that making any mistake is intolerable, that it's better to do nothing than to do something poorly, that anything less than success is failure) and leaves us directionless.

Naturally, our minds are desperate to rebuild coherence, so right now, you may be trying to rearrange all the pieces of the puzzle to get a nice, complete picture of what we want you to be doing. If you are, congratulations on being human and welcome to the coherence trap. Remember, we like things to make sense. We crave it. We like using logic and our problem-solving abilities—the same ones that produced touch-screen devices, space travel, machine intelligence, and smart homes—to fix inconsistencies in our stories. After all, if logic brought us the "Skip Intro" button on Netflix, what can't it do?

Well, it turns out that logic has limitations. Like Newton's law of universal gravitation, there are contexts in which a "universal" rule is inapplicable. For gravity, it's the quantum realm; for problem solving, it's (ironically) the mind. See for yourself. Don't think of a *pink tortoise*. Try really hard not to think of a *pink tortoise*, as if your pet's life depended on it. Convince yourself that it really is fine that you're constantly being evaluated. Don't feel bad about forgetting your mom's birthday, and definitely don't judge yourself for being a terrible human. If logic worked in your mind, you'd be able to fix these problems as effortlessly as you could turn up the heater when you feel cold or eat when you feel hungry. Unfortunately, you can't problem solve your way out of thoughts and feelings, no matter how smart you are.

Logic works only when you have control over the variables at play or over the variables that control the variables at play. For example, if X and Y cause Z and you want to get rid of Z, you can either directly eliminate Z, or, if you don't have control over Z, get rid of X and Y. If you don't like your wallpaper, tear it off. If you don't like the taste of garlic, omit it from the recipe. If you don't want to have the thought "I'm unlovable," throw it out. We're sure you'd do that if you could, except changing your thoughts is different from changing your wallpaper or anything else in the physical world. So, if you're feeling nervous about the toast you'll be giving at your brother's wedding, do you really believe you can "reason" your way to feeling confident? We doubt it; you need something other than logic to address perfectionism.

The alternative to logic or coherence is function. Focus on whether thoughts *work for you* and listen to them based on that. Act as if the *truth* of thoughts matters less than their *helpfulness*. This doesn't mean you suddenly become an uncritical consumer of information; that would be *unhelpful* (for the most part). Rather, it's decreasing the value you reflexively place on accuracy over utility. Useful thoughts are more like cheerleaders than jeering fans; they help you get to where you want to be. When you tell yourself "I've got this" right before giving a presentation, you don't know whether that's true, but it's probably helpful. What's true may not be helpful (for instance, "Everyone can see the sweat stains on my shirt"), and what's helpful may not always be true ("No one is looking at my sweat stains"). Would you rather listen to thoughts that unconditionally want the best for you or ones that care only about being right? What does being right do for you in the grand scheme of things?

If it's difficult to see thoughts in this light, imagine them as well-intentioned strangers. Say you're late to an important meeting, and the train you're riding breaks down. This stranger might say, "You're going to be in so much trouble. This is the third meeting you'll be late for in two weeks." Is it true? Maybe. Is it helpful? Unlikely. If you took those statements seriously, you'd probably be left panicking on the stationary train. What if the stranger were to say, "Hey, I'm sorry this is happening right now, especially with all the stress you've been dealing with at home"? That's probably more helpful. It'd be wonderful if your mind were naturally calm and validating, but that's not what it was programmed to do. It was designed to keep you alive by problem solving when things go wrong—the sooner, the better. That's why your thoughts can feel pressing and urgent, and why you're so instinctively pulled to act on them—at one point, our lives literally depended on it.

Acknowledging Without Surrendering

Regardless of the evolutionary might of thoughts and feelings, *thoughts and feelings don't cause behaviors*. As much as you've been conditioned to believe that they do—by businesses selling "positive thinking" and cultural messaging that says changing our attitude solves life problems—thoughts and feelings cannot make you do anything. Intuitively, you know this: just because you believe you can do something doesn't mean you can. A child who's convinced they can fly is no more likely to be airborne. This is the same reason why you can't "will" yourself to change. You can't just conjure up "willpower" and expect behaviors to follow. Behaviors happen only when you *do* them. Conversely, just because you think you can't do something doesn't make it so, like when you tell yourself you can't have another potato chip or can't procrastinate again. Remember, it's obedience to the thoughts—not the thoughts themselves—that's powerful.

It turns out that while you can't control whether thoughts show up, how long they stay, how loud they yell, or when they leave, you can choose *what* you do with them. The following sections outline four possible responses to try out the next time a well-worn, unwanted thought shows up: listen, acknowledge, watch, and consider.

Listen. You already know how to listen to your thoughts, especially rules. "I need to compensate for slacking off this weekend by working extra today." This thought appears, and you work through midnight as the blue light from your uncaring computer screen burns your eyes. "I can't turn in mediocre work." You watch a deadline pass without submitting the largely completed project you have sitting on your desktop. "Every thank-you note I write has to be thoughtful and personal." It's now two years after your wedding, and you haven't sent a single note out because none of them are sufficiently thoughtful and personal. We don't need to teach you how to listen better.

Acknowledge. Acknowledge your thoughts as thoughts. See them for what they are: sounds strung together into intelligible words (thanks to your language abilities) and products of your history and current circumstances. Thoughts and rules are arbitrary. They can't do anything to you if you don't listen to them; they're equivalent to the tiny man cowering behind the green curtain, the floor lava you cling to the couch to avoid, the prankster's WET PAINT sign on a dry wall.

From this perspective, appreciate the pull your thoughts have over you. Notice how strongly you experience the thought "I'm not good enough" or the rule "I can't afford to mess up" and how these syllables elicit sadness, jealousy, shame, and fear—just as the letters B-R-O-K-E-N on an elevator door can send you trudging up seven flights of stairs even if the elevator is actually working. Your immediate instinct to listen and obey before questioning is why the ability to pause and notice the sound of a thought—before attending to its content—is so crucial; it slows the automatic process of, well, taking thoughts at their word.

Treating perfectionistic thoughts seriously is similar to trying to get someone with different political views to agree with you: before you know it, you're already knee-deep in pointless arguing. Instead, assess whether it's worth spending your energy on this debate. It may be tempting to respond to verbal bait (metaphor inspired by a line from Hannah Gadsby's 2020 stand-up comedy special *Douglas*), like "climate change," "police brutality," "anti-vaccination," "universal health care," "failure," "loser," "perfect," and "successful." Don't take the bait.

Look past the bait. Look to your goals and values: What do *you* want to do with your time and energy? If you decide that your mental and emotional resources would be better spent doing anything other than arguing, do something else. Nod politely, acknowledge that the person has words to say, and exit the conversation. You can do the same with your thoughts: acknowledge them ("Yes, I see you're making sounds"), and then redirect your attention to something more worthy of your time and energy.

Watch. Acknowledging thoughts as thoughts, in turn, allows you to watch thinking as an ongoing, primarily self-driven activity, like watching someone launch into a political rant, only you don't get caught up in buzzwords or engage with them. You're not capitulating to or agreeing with them; your stance doesn't change. It's more like watching the person's fists clench, veins protrude through skin, volume crescendo, and shoulders tense, as if you were David Attenborough watching lions on the savanna. As loud or upset as the person is, you can continue to watch dispassionately, even curiously. Leave the bait where it is.

The dispassionate part is important; it means you're indifferent to the outcome. You don't root for the lions or their prey. To use a sports analogy, it's like watching a game in which your team isn't playing. As much as I, Clarissa, love the San Antonio Spurs, watching them play can be harrowing. I care about who has the ball, who's having an off night, what the referees are doing, and how close Coach Pop is to getting ejected. Sometimes, I find myself cursing out a referee or yelling at the TV screen, to no avail. As much as I want to control the outcome of the game, I can't. But watching the Golden State Warriors play the Milwaukee Bucks is painless (not for Mike, who's from Wisconsin) because I don't care who wins. I don't care who gets a technical, and I don't care who blows a fourth-quarter lead.

Try watching your thoughts as a dispassionate viewer rather than a zealous fan. Relinquish the stakes you think you have in the game (my life doesn't change even if the Spurs don't make the playoffs) and let go of trying to influence outcomes beyond your control. What happens when you absolve yourself of the responsibility of regulating your thoughts and feelings? No more trying to kick the "I'm not good enough" thought off the court, begging "I'm worthy" to keep playing, relegating "I need to work harder" to the bench, or exiling "No one likes me" to the locker room. Instead of corralling and coaxing, let the players go wherever and do whatever they want, because, ultimately, who wins (which thought is the last one standing) doesn't need to affect your quality of life.

Another way to put this is: watch the process of *thinking*, not thoughts. Watching thoughts is getting nervous when Thanos finds the Avengers; watching thinking is appreciating how intricate Josh Brolin's makeup is and how realistic the special effects and CGI are. Watch the process, not the product.

Practice this. For sixty seconds, acknowledge your thoughts as thoughts (give them a metaphorical wave if you want) and watch thinking do its thing. See if you can notice its speed, volume, cadence, rhythm, whether it flows smoothly or leaps from idea to idea, and if it's visual or verbal.

...

...

...

What was it like to watch thinking happen? Write down any observations in your notebook. Were you able to watch thinking dispassionately—even curiously—as if the results of the game didn't matter?

Consider. Another possible response is to consider what your thoughts have to say, because listening to your thoughts now and again can be useful. Considering your thoughts requires you to first recognize that you don't have to do what they tell you. Your mind is like that aunt of yours who may not know exactly what's going on in your life but still tries to give you advice. Most of the time, her advice does not apply to your specific situation even if she sounds generically helpful, and indiscriminately taking her advice may set you down a path she thinks you want, not the one you actually want. Still, there are times when your thoughts come through with the insight you need to navigate your present challenges. Those times, you're better off listening to them.

The key is to discern when to listen. Assess the situation with respect to your goals and determine if the advice your thoughts are giving you will serve you in attaining those goals. Let's say you're struggling with breaking up with a friend and your aunt says, "Just ignore their texts and they'll take the hint." If you care about being a kind person, you probably wouldn't follow her advice. But what if she says, "Just be honest. It's going to be hard either way, but that's probably what you'd want a friend to do for you"? In this case, if you care about being open and honest, take her advice. You can treat thoughts and rules similarly, as advice that can be ignored or followed, depending on your struggles, needs, goals, and values.

Another reason to consider thoughts is that they provide you with valuable data, if you know where to look. For example, at face value, the statement "I like being around people" may reflect your interpersonal preferences. It signals that you're an extrovert. But on a deeper level, these words may reveal a fear of loneliness or a need for external validation. A simpler example is: "I want dessert." It could mean you want dessert, or it could mean you use sugar and carbs as a means of emotion regulation. You can use what thoughts are *trying* to tell you—not what they're saying—to inform your decisions. Thus, maybe next time, you won't have extra dessert in order to stave off developing a pattern of emotional eating. Similarly, you can choose to face your fear of being alone (we'll talk about how to do this in the next chapter) rather than surround yourself with people to hide from this fear.

Think for Yourself

The function of acknowledging thoughts as thoughts, watching thinking as automatic and perpetually in motion, and considering thoughts and rules as potential sources of wisdom (they may be rubbish) is to give yourself more room to maneuver around them. Instead of defaulting to listening to and obeying your thoughts, practicing these other responses to them gives you more options. Instead of arguing with your political contrarian buddy, you can tune them out, notice the color of their shirt, or take their constructive points and ignore everything else they say. How much easier would your life be if you could simply step out of the mental circus as and when you pleased or if you could easily disengage when engaging didn't serve you? Imagine what you could invest that time and effort into. Seriously, take a few seconds to contemplate all the rule following, arguing, reasoning, justifying, rationalizing, validating, denying, reassuring, and surrendering. Weigh all that. Now picture yourself being relieved of all that weight. Sit with the lightness. Where will you go from here?

Write down in your notebook the activities you'd be redirecting your energy toward. Notice if your mind is meticulously evaluating all the possible options—even before you write anything down—trying to get you to pick "productive" activities. Practice simply acknowledging your perfectionistic mind attempting to be helpful and let yourself list whatever activities you want, no matter how ludicrous or lazy your mind says they are: learning to dance *The Nutcracker* ballet, sleeping, raking leaves, making a sourdough starter, Rollerblading. Let go of the judgments. See what that opens up.

*   *   *

Perfectionism exerts power over your behaviors using rules and reasons. It tells you what you *should* do and *why*. However, these rules are arbitrary and can't actually make you do anything, no matter how strongly they're worded or how loudly they're said. Therefore, when perfectionism threatens you with a life of failure for getting a B on an assignment or breaking off a long-term relationship, you can't take it at its word.

Instead, we encourage you to (1) acknowledge your thoughts as thoughts—nothing more, nothing less; (2) watch thinking as it occurs in real time, as if you have no stakes in what happens next; and (3) consider what your thoughts have to say, then take what's helpful and ignore the rest. You can circumvent the trap of perfectionism by focusing on thoughts that work toward your goals (function) rather than those that make sense or seem true (coherence).

In the next chapter, we'll turn to how to make space for the discomfort that naturally accompanies flouting rules and generally being less than perfect.

CHAPTER 4

Making Room for Feelings of Imperfection

Being alive is hard. Life contains pain, suffering, and imperfection. Although we can try to deny our flaws, rejecting any part of our existence only makes our lives narrower. Moreover, avoiding confronting our innate failings and the feelings that accompany them forces us to withdraw when we don't feel (insert fitting word: "good," "successful," "attractive," "competent," "smart," what have you), closing ourselves off from the fullness of life.

We know imperfection doesn't feel good. That's why perfectionism is addictive. You not only get rewarded for performing well in the form of trophies, praise, money, and virtual likes (positive reinforcement; see chapter 2 for an explanation), but you also get rid of the uncomfortable sense of "not good enough" (negative reinforcement; also discussed in chapter 2). It's a win-win. And it's not just "not good enough." You also don't have to feel like a failure, overwhelmed, ashamed, anxious, stressed, worried, guilty, lazy, unproductive, annoyed, frustrated, and self-hating. Your problem-solving mind infers that being perfect will eliminate all these unpleasant feelings. What does your actual experience tell you about this line of reasoning?

The Origin of Feelings

Feelings have been and still are crucial to our survival. They motivate us to act in ways that increase our chances of staying alive. Fear tells us to run from predators, shame keeps us in line with the in-group, hunger drives us to search for food, disgust deters us from eating toxic substances, and so on. The evolutionary advantages of feelings make us uniquely sensitive to them, so we respond to them automatically and quickly. In fact, if the humans who were most reactive to fear were the ones most capable of saving themselves from predators (because they'd rather bolt than risk getting eaten), then it's *by design* that the ones of us who are left have inherited that reactivity. That's why anxiety, stress, and worry affect us so much.

Although feelings were originally adaptive, our world and our culture have evolved more rapidly than our biology (Hayes and Sanford 2014). Yes, feelings still tell us important things about our current situation, like if we're in danger, but we weren't designed to live with constantly updating social media feeds, implausible beauty standards, capitalist cravings, or screen-mediated interactions. The discrepancy between nature's plans and the world we now inhabit means that feelings are more likely to provide false signals and instigate behaviors inconsistent with our goals. Thus, even though fear will show up when you're walking along the edge of a cliff (arguably adaptive), it's also going to show up when you scroll through social media posts and see your friends having fun without you (fear of missing out) or when you don't color in the right bubble on a piece of paper (fear of failing).

These misplaced feelings create distress that compromises our well-being rather than saves us from demise, so we need to sort helpful from unhelpful feelings and act on them selectively. For example, it may be helpful to act on pain in your hamstring during exercise to prevent injury but not act on social anxiety when you're trying to make new friends. Base your choices on the helpful feelings.

Your Feelings Are Valid

The validity of feelings is independent of their utility; just because feelings haven't caught up to your current needs and goals doesn't make them less valid. Your feelings are de facto valid. By "valid," we don't mean they need to be responded to, dealt with, or justified (that's the coherence trap); we mean they get to exist. That's it.

This concept probably contradicts what you've learned over the years. Since you were tiny, you've needed to arm yourself with explanations for your feelings. "Why are you crying?" "Why are you so anxious?" "You have no reason to be upset." Not only are you expected to defend your feelings, but your reasons also have to be satisfactory to the asker (who happens to adore coherence). Somehow, other people get to judge whether *your* feelings are valid, as if you're permitted to have feelings only when society deems them appropriate for the situation. Otherwise, you're "uptight," "dramatic," "sensitive," "needy," "crazy," or "broken."

That's unfair. Your feelings are allowed to be as big or as small, as dull or as vibrant, and as light or as heavy as they are. If you accept the premise that feelings are unconditionally acceptable and valid, then statements like "You need to calm down," "Cheer up," and "You're overreacting" become absurd, as if one were commenting that a sunset should be pinker or leaves should be greener. When you give feelings permission to exist, you give yourself permission to *experience* feelings by extension. And if you're allowed to feel whatever shows up, then why would you suppress your feelings or apologize for their presence?

Emotional Avoidance

Evolutionarily, it makes sense that your instinct is to avoid, control, or escape from unpleasant feelings. Avoiding physical dangers has kept humans safe over the years, so logic reasons that you can also do this for the threats inside your head. Only you know that's inaccurate, because your experiences indicate otherwise. They tell you that you can't outrun your feelings, no matter how hard you try. You may have forestalled stress by watching *The Great British Bake Off*, but it comes right back once the episode ends—usually even stronger. You may even be able to assuage worry by enumerating reasons for its irrationality, but how long does the quiet last? Either the same worry returns under a new guise or a different worry takes its place. Emotional avoidance doesn't work in the long term.

In addition, emotional avoidance *shrinks* the space in which life happens. The more you avoid, the less space you have to live your life. If everything is dangerous, nothing is safe. So you find a corner that appears untouched by threat and take shelter there, hoping nothing scary comes a-knocking. This is isolating yourself to avoid fear of judgment, pushing away people to avoid fear of intimacy, and erasing yourself to avoid feeling like a burden. Yet pain still finds you, because trying to avoid feelings as a human is like trying to avoid getting wet when you go swimming in the ocean. Recall the last time you didn't feel anything, not even numbness. When you try to avoid the unavoidable, necessary pain turns into unnecessary suffering. You hurt even more—all because you're trying to live a life free of pain.

But maybe you're not trying to avoid *all* feelings, just *bad* ones, which is like saying you're not trying to avoid *all* waves, just *bad* ones. Unfortunately, you don't get to pick and choose which waves crash down on you. If you're swimming in the ocean, you're exposing yourself to all of it. There may be waves you like more than others and are more willing to get drenched by, but your preferences are unrelated to which waves show up and how much control you have over them. Meanwhile, is swimming in the ocean still fun if you're constantly evaluating each wave and hoping only good ones will roll your way? To truly enjoy swimming in the ocean, you need to be willing to experience all the waves.

Clarifying Acceptance

"Be open to discomfort." "Sit with stress." "Accept anxious feelings." You may have heard some version of these directives before. They get at the idea that making room for feelings is more helpful than trying to shut them out of your life. That's easier said than done. In a way, you're going against your biology by refraining from reacting to signals of danger. If we lived in prehistoric times, the hippies who make peace with their thoughts and emotions would be the first to be eaten. But we're way past that era now.

Before we get to how to practice emotional openness, let's understand why: Why would you choose to make room for unpleasant feelings when you have the option to eliminate them? The first reason is obvious: you *don't* have the option to get rid of unpleasant feelings—you know this based on experience. The second reason is: because doing the opposite—forcing out imperfection, being hypervigilant about anything less than "good," criticizing yourself for insignificant mistakes, snapping at people who fall short of your standards—is tiring and self-sabotaging. The third reason is that pain clarifies what matters to you deep down. When you hurt from rejection, pain is telling you that you care about connection. When you feel angered by structural inequity, the message is that you care about social justice. You can't be hurt by things you don't care about, and you can't turn off the hurt without turning off the caring.

Making room for feelings you don't like means getting good at *feeling* distress (emphasis on the verb). The issue might be that you're bad at having feelings in the first place, because if you've been constantly running from emotions, you don't *feel* them. That is, you've gotten tons of practice avoiding and much less practice being with feelings as they are. Imagine if you got good at *feeling* distress. This means that whenever distress barges into your life, you can simply feel it, unperturbed, and continue on with whatever you were doing wherever you are.

This is *acceptance*. "Acceptance" is a dicey term because it's been used in so many contexts, including being synonymous with "resignation." We *accept* defeat and losses. We *accept* punishment. However, in this context, we mean "accept" like "receive." We *accept* the kindness and generosity of strangers. We *accept* well wishes and presents. So, too, we *accept* anxiety, stress, and worry. If we can make room in our lives for meetings that could have been done via email, we can make room for thoughts and feelings we don't like.

To practice acceptance, first clarify exactly what it is that you're accepting. We're *not* asking you to accept failure or some wretched fate. Unlike emotions, you have some control over those consequences. Dr. Steven Hayes said it eloquently: "It's about accepting your history and capacity to feel, not your situations or behaviors" (this quote is from a workshop he presented in 2020 titled "ACT as a Form of Process-Based Therapy: Introduction and Beyond"). In other words, we're asking you to accept that your feelings originate from your cumulative experiences on this earth and to accept—even marvel at—your unique human ability to experience and label an incredible range of emotions. It's pretty amazing that you can discriminate between forlorn and miserable or frustrated and annoyed (though there might be some semantic hairsplitting involved). Ultimately, you have some power to change your situation (your privilege determines the extent to which this is true) and choose different actions, but your history and feelings are what they are.

Making Room for Feelings

Accepting and being willing to have feelings means giving feelings space to exist, just like you might make space in your living room for an ugly piece of furniture inherited from your grandparents. Accepting is not liking; accepting is giving space. In contrast, when you reject feelings—these products of your history—you necessarily reject yourself, because you are made from your history. Emotional avoidance is self-invalidation from within.

Practice *feeling* uncomfortable. (You can access an audio recording of this "Feeling Uncomfortable" exercise at http://www.newharbinger.com/48459.) Wherever you are reading this, shift into an awkward position. Maybe slump down onto the mattress if you're on your bed, lean over the side of the couch, or roll over if you're on the floor. Remain in place for the rest of the exercise. Once you're in position:

1. See if you can notice which part of your body feels most uncomfortable. Is it your shoulders, neck, lower back, jaw, legs, or chest? Find the spot that stands out. Gently bring your attention to it. Don't try to change or control the feeling in any way.

2. Give it a face (it doesn't have to be a literal face, just a representative visual). What does the discomfort look like? What is its shape, color, size, expression, density, and so forth?

3. Observe how it's moving (or not moving). Is it pacing up and down, radiating from its core, pinballing in all directions, pulsing like a wave, or staying completely still?

4. Trace the boundary of the feeling in your body. Follow it to where it ends and draw a perimeter around it. Take a mental step back and look at the space in which this feeling is existing. Don't do anything with it. Just look.

5. When you have a sense of the entirety of the feeling, watch it as if it were a movie. Watch the frame change from second to second, letting the feeling do its thing. Your job is to watch, not to rewind or fast-forward. Bring some curiosity to the watching—as if you've never felt this feeling before. What's it going to do next? Where's it going to go? What other parts of your body is it reaching?

6. After you've watched the feeling for a while—to the point that you could describe it to someone else—look for something new about the feeling you hadn't noticed earlier. Maybe it's showing

up in a new place. Maybe it has alternating rhythms. Maybe it has a layer of heaviness to it.

7. Return to step 5: Watch the feeling as you now know it as if it's playing on a theater screen. Get cozy in your mind's armchair and watch the show for a few moments.

What was it like to make room for discomfort? In your notebook, jot down words or phrases describing the experience. Note what was useful or not useful about being open to the feeling.

If you were able to watch the discomfort with curiosity, without trying to alter it in any way by moving your body, you've just practiced acceptance. What you did was give the feeling space to exist on its own terms. We recommend practicing this sequence in other situations when you notice discomfort. For example, if you're feeling stressed about picking a place for dinner, go through the steps. Feel the stress, watch it, and make room for it.

If you found it difficult to stay in the exercise, that sounds about right. Accepting is a skill. Like any other skill, it gets easier with practice. If you've never touched a ramekin, you're not going to make a beautifully airy soufflé on your first attempt, but that doesn't mean you never will. It may feel like acceptance is impossible or far away (there's the mental noise again). So what? Just as you didn't have to move your body to cave to discomfort, you don't have to take a naysaying thought seriously.

If you found the exercise extremely easy, that's also great. Perhaps this isn't a new concept to you, or you're naturally gifted—keep doing what you're doing. However, check if you were subtly avoiding discomfort. Like rules and reasons, avoidance is all around you, so you may not even realize when you're avoiding. Before you can accept, you need to be aware of avoidance and curtail it. As long as you're avoiding in any way, acceptance becomes an empty performance rather than genuine practice; even if you're technically doing all the moves, you won't get better at the skill.

Practicing acceptance (or any other skill in this book) is like learning how to weight lift. When you're first building strength, form is critical. It's not just about picking up a barbell off the floor and heaving it over your head. You need to engage the right muscles and use the right motions. This is the form that will eventually help you lift a three-hundred-pound barbell. Executing poor form only risks injury and limits your potential. In fact, it's even more crucial to practice good form with lighter weights so that you get into the habit of lifting a certain way. You also need to be able to independently discern when you're using correct versus incorrect technique, because you won't always have someone monitoring you. Translated back to acceptance, this means knowing when you're avoiding feelings versus actively welcoming feelings, even if you don't like them.

Avoidance looks different for everyone. A sign of avoidance is relief when the exercise is over. If you were tolerating the discomfort with an eye on the clock, that's avoidance, like wrapping yourself up in plastic to go swimming so you don't get wet. You weren't fully giving the feeling space to be present. Without consciously doing so, you set conditions for the existence of the feeling: it can stay as long as it leaves once the exercise is over. This is the emotional equivalent of constantly stewing over the obnoxious magenta ottoman in your living room, counting down the days to when you can finally donate it. Wouldn't it be easier if you could let it be there as its gaudy self—even if it is an eyesore—so you can immerse yourself in the cinematic greatness of *Watchmen*?

Alternatively, if you felt completely comfortable during the exercise, that could also be avoidance. Maybe you reshaped the discomfort into something you could bear. You accepted it because you *made* it acceptable. This is like telling your partner you love them exactly as they are as you fervently encourage them to revamp their wardrobe, pick up "more interesting" hobbies, and learn to cook like Julia Child. If you loved your partner exactly as they are, they wouldn't need to keep doing more to impress you, just as discomfort doesn't need to be something different for you to make room for it.

As you try out different methods of accepting, you'll land on one that feels unfamiliar. The moment of recognition is hard to describe, but it could be realizing that you're not fighting, can take a breath, and can unconditionally let the feeling be. Even if the stance feels strange, it might also feel lighter in some ways, as if you could keep it up for a while. That's how you know you're getting closer to acceptance; it'll feel *sustainable*.

Unlike an athletic or scholastic skill, you can practice acceptance no matter what you're doing. Any time you feel *something*, practice. You can even try it out with pleasant feelings, though you're probably pretty good at that already. We tend to readily be open to feelings we like but don't extend the courtesy to feelings we label as "bad." So, if you're feeling impatient at an especially long red light, practice. Feeling frustrated by a coworker who missed their deadline for the third time in a row? Practice. Feeling stressed about the email from your boss you received six minutes ago to which you still haven't replied? Practice. Feeling overwhelmed by the mountain of yardwork you need to tackle over the weekend? Make room for that feeling, then start acting from wherever it makes sense for you and your goals.

Accepting is giving feelings room to exist so you can focus on things that matter to you, rather than be preoccupied with when the feeling is going to leave. All this practice is *for you*; we're not into suffering for the sake of suffering. There needs to be a purpose to doing hard work, so it's worth asking: If you never had to spend another second worrying about whether, how long, or how much discomfort showed up, what would that mean for you?

❀　❀　❀

Feelings are part of being human. You can't escape them no matter how hard you try. Part of why they're so stubborn is that they've been historically adaptive, so it has been in your favor to act on them. However, this assumption doesn't hold in many situations today. Thus, even though your feelings are always valid and sometimes helpful, you need to recognize when to heed their advice and when to let them throw a tantrum in the background. By letting them fuss without giving them more attention than necessary, you're practicing acceptance.

The target of acceptance is feelings, not behaviors or situations. Acceptance entails watching your feelings—even and especially unpleasant ones—as if you were watching a movie you've never seen before. As you practice making room for unpleasant feelings, catch yourself when you're subtly avoiding, and then go back to watching. Recognize when watching feels sustainable; that means you're getting closer to acceptance.

Now that you've worked on acknowledging thoughts and feelings without ceding control of your life to them, we'll turn to what to do with the labels and stories you have about yourself, the ones that tell you who you can and cannot be.

CHAPTER 5

Letting Go of Your Labels and Stories

How would you describe yourself? Take out your notebook and write down three words that come to mind. Briefly recount a story that illustrates each descriptor. For example, if one of your adjectives was "reliable," you might think of the time your friend's car broke down in the middle of the night and you drove an hour to rescue them. If you wrote "organized," you might think of all the systems you created to keep your home or office running smoothly.

Notice how easily you came up with those labels. All of us do this all the time. We're "anxious," "depressed," "neat," "nice," "hardworking," "smart"—we're perpetually defining ourselves with labels. We do the same thing with other people: Walter is a "sociopath," Skyler has "fortitude," Jesse has a "good heart," Marie is "loyal," Saul is a "coward." Constructing narratives for yourself and others is part of the coherence trap (see chapter 3). You create a logical map so that you know how elements of the story fit together and how to respond to them appropriately.

In your notebook, outline how each label you assigned yourself influences your behaviors and perspectives. Maybe because you're an "introvert," you skip parties. Because you have a "good work ethic," you sacrifice quality time with your family to get work done. Because you "care about succeeding," spending time on anything other than your goals means you're "lazy."

The issue is not that you readily give yourself labels—it's that the labels dictate what you do and how you view yourself and the world. That's why we're going to take a closer look at them, so you can choose the extent to which they shape your life.

Clarifying Self-Labels and Self-Stories

Self-labels are anything you use to describe yourself. They can be identities, like "feminist," "morning person," "gay," "worrier," or "perfectionist." They can also be more elaborate accounts or *self-stories*. Self-stories don't have to be accurate; they're just how you see yourself. Stories are a way to string labels together into a coherent narrative: I "love nature," so I'm "always going hiking, backpacking, and climbing." Self-stories encompass almost every way we see ourselves, including criticisms: I'm "never going to reach my goals" because I'm a "loser" who "can't do anything right." Self-labels and self-stories get folded into the rules and reasons perfectionism uses to keep you in line. I "should" be able to meet all of my children's needs because I'm a "good parent."

Most of us have a core self-story that runs through almost every nook and cranny of our existence. This is the self-story you find yourself coming back to constantly, no matter what you're doing. The self-story could be something like, "I deserve to be alone," "There's something wrong with me," or "Deep down, I'm a bad person." When you contemplate the reason behind your rejecting affection, preemptively ending relationships, neglecting self-care, chasing burnout, seeking approval from authority figures, and so on, you might find that these actions are all linked to your belief that you are fundamentally unlovable. If you walk through life believing that (or another similar story), how could you *not* struggle with self-acceptance?

Although we have described these concepts separately here, the distinction between label and story is more form than function, which means, how you view and interact with self-labels and self-stories matters more than how many words they contain.

When Self-Labels and Self-Stories Become Problematic

Like thoughts and feelings, self-labels and self-stories aren't harmful in and of themselves. It's your *interactions* with them that detract from the life you want. This happens when you take a label seriously and constrain your activities to fit the label. Sometimes this is helpful, and other times it's not. For example, if you think of yourself as a "good friend" and that leads you to be supportive when you feel frustrated with your friends, then following the "good friend" label in those situations is constructive. However, trying to fulfill the "good friend" label by providing emotional support to a friend when you're mired in depression may be counterproductive. When that happens, pause, recalibrate, and determine what move will be most helpful given your goals and values, independent of labels and stories.

Self-labels and self-stories can become problematic if, (1) you choose your behaviors based on what they tell you; (2) your attachment to them leads to unnecessary suffering; or (3) you conflate your labels with your experiences. When we talk about attachment to labels or stories (as in the second scenario here), we're referring to rigid adherence to their content and implicit expectations, such that everything you do or believe must line up with the label or story. Hence, if you accept the label "broken," then you can't seek out—and certainly don't deserve—any healthy reciprocal relationship, so you deprive yourself of meaningful connections.

When self-labels govern behavior. If your actions are determined by your labels, they may be decoupled from your goals and values. For instance, you might choose to attend medical school so you can be—or because you are—"smart" rather than because you're moved to be in a helping profession. Consequently, you may feel dissatisfied your entire career because being labeled "smart" isn't actually what nourishes your soul. Or maybe you're so attached to being a "caregiver" that you plan, check in, and micromanage even when your family members are resistant. In this example, you may be unknowingly eroding these treasured relationships to be consistent with your "caregiver" label. When you give precedence to the coherence of self-stories over the effect they have, you end up choosing what makes sense to your mind instead of what improves your well-being and that of those around you.

When self-labels create suffering. Even if your attachment to labels doesn't significantly influence your behaviors, it can still be detrimental. When you're firmly attached to labels, inconsistencies become jarring and can elicit feelings of self-doubt, frustration, hopelessness, insecurity, and shame *beyond* what is necessary—this is suffering. For example, if you "value social justice," then you should always be examining your privilege, using it in ways that benefit underserved groups, taking actions that advance equity, supporting sustainable agriculture, purchasing from small businesses, educating yourself on the news, voting in local elections, and so on. Any deviation from these actions means you're "hypocritical," "selfish," and a "bad person." Accordingly, you may feel pressured to do all the right things and experience guilt when you inevitably fail to be fully congruent with your label.

Moreover, when you're inundated by these difficult emotions, you may end up doing nothing, because starting anything feels overwhelming. In this way, labels keep you in a rut. Following your labels to the letter is like being at a buffet where you're expected to eat everything. Although trying some soup and a couple of desserts would be great, the burden of eating the extensive array of food is paralyzing.

As explained in the previous chapter, the unpleasant feelings that stem from having labels are de facto acceptable and valid. They are part of your experience; therefore, they are valid. However, you can opt out of the struggle and suffering born out of attachment to your labels ("I value social justice, so that means I *must…*") when you hold them more lightly. Being flexible with your labels means you take the food you want from the buffet and leave what your stomach doesn't have room for *at this point*; the buffet of life will still be there whenever you choose to return.

When self-labels cloud reality. When labels gain a stronghold in your perception of yourself and the world, you can lose sight of what is *actually* happening and instead believe what your labels say *should be* happening. Let's say you label yourself an "introvert," which to you means that you don't like being around new people. This self-label asserts that you must have loathed being at that party where everyone was immersed in conversation about their work and families. Yet your experience at the party might tell you that you actually enjoyed learning about the three dogs Charles adopted after his divorce or the dance troupe Gina founded.

When you need stories to be coherent (for instance, introverts don't like parties), you allow labels to override your lived experience and you miss what's occurring in the moment. This also happens when you deny feeling sad about a breakup because you're "glad" your ex-partner has moved on, even though both feelings are true to your experience. Ultimately, tunnel vision on labels and stories that are intended to make sense of the world paradoxically prevents you from living your life story *as it is happening.*

The good news is that attachment to self-labels and self-stories is a *choice.* You can choose to live in the alternate reality your mind has conjured or in the world as it is. If you want to live by your experiences instead of your labels, practice perspective taking.

Perspective Taking from a Self Without Labels

Who are you without your labels? Take a second to ponder that. Drop all the adjectives and nouns after "I am…" and see what's left. Just be "I" for a few moments. Settle into what it's like to simply be, without identities clouding your perception. No "neurotic," "accomplished," "funny," "ambitious," "sensitive," and such. Just be. Survey your mind space from this vantage point.

   ...

   ...

   ...

What did you notice when you let go of your labels? Perhaps you felt a new lightness without the need to prove yourself. Perhaps you discovered you could be truly present without these anchors (in a way, labels and stories are designed to anchor us—to keep us consistent). Maybe you felt uncertain and confused. Maybe you felt distressed when you couldn't find a way to simply be. We're hoping that whatever you noticed, it was a change from your typical experience, because that illustrates how strongly your experiences are colored by labels and stories—and opens up an alternative possibility in which you choose differently.

Like removing blinders, letting go of self-identities exposes you to the whole of your reality, not just the parts that cohere with your established narratives. For example, maybe you love listening to obscure artists who sing about profound subjects *and* you genuinely relate to Taylor Swift, or you care a lot about striving for excellence *and* the most impressive accolades feel insubstantial, or you readily understand general relativity *and* you didn't realize your bicycle had gears until someone pointed them out. All these realities can coexist when you are free from your stories.

Now go a little further and let go of the self entirely. Whatever entity you see as your self, step back from that. Observe the thoughts, feelings, labels, and stories in the present space; watch them linger or drift by without attachment to these experiences or to a coherent self. What's it like to be detached from all of it, to be relieved of the burden of coherence?

Shifting from a self that is defined by the content of labels and stories to an observing (non)self entails a change in perspective, like looking at a towering mountain from the ground as opposed to looking at it from a plane in the sky. Even though the mountain doesn't change, it's experienced differently depending on your point of view. From the ground, you might view the mountain as an insurmountable behemoth that conjures feelings of fear and helplessness, but from the sky, you may see a stunning geological feature that reminds you of the beauty of nature and elicits calmness and awe. To be clear, perspective taking isn't about changing your mindset or attitude. That doesn't work—at least not where it really matters—so don't try to change the thoughts, feelings, or labels. Instead, take a different perspective on them. View them from the sky, not the ground.

Let's practice perspective taking (an audio version of this "Shifting Perspectives" exercise is available at http://www.newharbinger. com/48459). Start by bringing up labels in which you take some pride: "planner," "intelligent," "organized," "productive," "talented," "goal-oriented," "efficient"—whatever you identify with. Pick any of the labels.

Take a moment to observe *how* you view the label you selected. Where are you in relation to the label? How small or big is the label relative to you? Are you attached to it, indifferent, averse to it, scared, or excited? Are you looking at it from the ground or the sky?

. . .

. . .

. . .

Now float up to the clouds and look at the label from the sky (or if you were in the sky earlier, descend to the ground). What's it like to view the label from this other perspective? Notice how adjusting your perspective affects how you interact with the label. If this is tricky, try literally picturing the label as a mountain (or a building, lake, or tree) in the visualization as you toggle between ground and sky. The more details you can add to the visualization (like feeling the wind as you fly through the sky, feeling the solid ground beneath your feet), the easier it will be to stay engaged in the exercise. If this feels awkward, you're probably doing it right. Take a few moments to appreciate how your relationship with the label changes as you move your point of view.

Shifting perspectives is something most of us do naturally and automatically. For example, you can pretty easily put yourself in the shoes of a friend who waited forty minutes for you and can appreciate how frustrated they feel. You can probably also imagine how your dog feels being left alone at home most of the day while you're at work. You might even be able to grasp how the you of five years ago or the you five years from now would think of the present you. Our perspective-taking abilities transcend people, species, and time.

Evidently, perspective taking is familiar to you. You just tend not to use it with inner experiences. Taking a different perspective with your *self* may seem disorienting at first, especially if you've never practiced any form of mindfulness, but you'll quickly see that it's essentially similar to the perspective taking you do in your everyday life. Therefore, what you're training with this brand of perspective taking is *generalizing* the skill you already have by applying it to a new domain: your inner world. Instead of viewing the self as labels and stories, take the perspective of a (non)self who watches these labels and stories from the sky. Just as the sky is infinite and has room for all the mountains, oceans, deserts, forests, fjords, and icebergs—while not being defined by these features— so is the ever-expansive (non)self who is liberated from labels and stories.

Self-Criticism in Perfectionism

Self-criticism is a type of self-label or self-story, and all that we've talked about so far applies to it. However, it warrants its own discussion because of how pernicious it is in perfectionism. In many ways, self-criticism is the defining feature of perfectionism.

What are the self-criticisms you carry with you almost every day? For example, "I have no self-control," "I'm too anxious," "I overthink everything," "I don't belong," "Everyone thinks I'm incompetent," or "No one will ever love me." Identify three self-critical labels or stories you believe to be true about yourself and write them down in your notebook.

How long have you carried these self-criticisms with you? Pick the one you've grappled with the longest. Take yourself back to the first time you remember having this thought. How old were you? (Most people say they were really young.)

If the self-criticism showed up only recently (within the past couple of years), pick a different one. Sometimes, we avoid picking the heavy self-evaluations precisely because we see them as unconquerable mountains—so go for the big one. Recall your earliest memories with this self-criticism. Briefly describe them in your notebook.

...

...

...

Visualize a smaller version of you struggling with this thought. Where are you? What are you wearing? What are you feeling? What do you see, hear, and smell? Flesh out the scene with your five senses as much as possible, as if you were transported right back to that moment and you were right next to the smaller you.

...

...

...

What's it like to view your smaller self from your present perspective? Smaller you doesn't know any better. They believe the self-criticism to be their reality, not a story that's been foisted on them by forces outside their control (refer to chapter 1 for a discussion on the origins of perfectionism). This tiny person believes they are weak, unworthy, not good enough, difficult to be around, messed up, or unlovable for who they are.

See if you can appreciate the weight of the self-criticism they're carrying with them.

...

...

...

Can you see that this child was you? And that this child is *still* you? You might be bigger now, but the burden of these words has not abated. The self-criticism still eats away at you after all these years, and you haven't been able to extricate yourself from it. Where does that leave you?

The Effects of Self-Criticism

Self-criticism has the same power as self-labels and self-stories when you take it to be true; it controls your actions, creates unnecessary suffering, and distorts genuine experiences. Maybe you've worked yourself to the point of chronic back problems and migraines to prove your worth or sabotaged meaningful relationships because you're convinced you don't deserve them. When you believe there's something wrong with you at your core, you deny yourself the experience of being loved or savoring delightful moments.

Self-criticism is erosive; it wears you down so gradually that you may not even realize your life has contorted itself to satisfy its whims. Look at your life now. Compare it to the life you want to build for yourself. How much of what is missing has to do with believing the rhetoric of self-criticism? Perhaps you've dated only people who treat you poorly because self-criticism says you need to "settle for less." Or you've resigned yourself to what your life has been—the same boring hobbies, same passive-aggressive friends, same unfulfilling relationship, same mediocre job—rather than what it could be because you "can't do better." Or you're drained from trying to please everyone—constantly apologizing, saying yes, filtering your words—because you're "unlikable." It may not be immediately obvious, but once you start tracking the influence of self-criticism, you may be surprised (or not) to notice how much of your life is consumed by it. By buying into your inherent worthlessness, you've given self-criticism the power to dictate the boundaries of your existence. It's the self-story that keeps on taking.

In your notebook, list a few things you've done or not done because of self-criticism. Reflect on how believing self-criticism has taken a toll on your well-being and how it affects what your life looks like today.

Using Self-Criticism as Motivation

Your mind might be protesting right now, contending that self-criticism can be helpful, like when it provides you with motivation. It says you wouldn't have gotten as far as you have if you didn't motivate yourself with criticism. You need to tell yourself you're not good enough in order to perform well, the story goes. Well, as therapists who have worked with scores of people who have struggled with self-criticism, we want to emphatically dispel the myth that self-criticism is necessary fuel for success. It is just as likely that you berated yourself *and* you accomplished the things you set out to accomplish. That is, they both happened, and one didn't cause the other. Plus, even if this story is accurate—that you routinely tell yourself you aren't good enough and you subsequently work harder to prove the criticism wrong—is that really how you would want your life to go?

Apply that means of motivation to anyone you care about: a sibling, friend, parent, child, partner. Picture yourself trying to get your younger sibling to study harder by telling them they're worthless or telling your child that they'll be an unemployed deadbeat if they don't finish their math homework. Picture yourself doing that and observe the feelings that show up. We're guessing you feel icky inside; using censure to spur action seems needlessly cruel. Yet you do this to yourself every day when you use self-criticism as fuel. "You're a terrible person for not making your bed." "You need to stop being a burden on your family."

Not only does self-criticism make you miserable, but you'd probably still pursue the things you care about even without the nonstop mind lashings—if only because you care about them. Would you really lose your job if you didn't shame yourself for making mistakes at work? Would you leave your children starving and unkempt if you stopped believing you're a "bad parent"? If these are the consequences of excising self-criticism, then it might be worth assessing how much you care about those goals in the first place. Have you been trying to prove a point or to live your best life?

Another issue with following the rule that you need self-criticism to excel is that you've probably never tried it the other way. People can go their whole lives doing something ineffectively because it works well enough, eschewing more fruitful alternatives. Perhaps, even without self-criticism, you'd perform just as well—or better—and your overall quality of life would improve. As you venture into uncertain territory, perfectionism will caution you against the slew of negative outcomes it expects you to face once you take your foot off the self-criticism pedal; that's more coherence at work, like never visiting a restaurant because a friend told you the food was subpar. Connect with the part of you that wants to experience life as it is, not as your mind says it should be. Decide whether you want self-criticism to be the primary driving force in your life or if you want something different. Take a risk. See what living for yourself can be like.

❀   ❀   ❀

We all do it. We use labels and stories to define ourselves and, correspondingly, the actions we can and cannot take: a "nerd" doesn't do sports, a "conscientious" person always checks their work, a "nice" person never says no. In perfectionism, these labels and stories are usually critical: "useless," "stupid," "incompetent," "unlovable." When we're rigidly attached to these labels, they influence our behaviors, create unnecessary suffering, and warp our perception of ourselves and the world—all to our detriment.

In this chapter, we advocated taking the perspective of an observing (non)self with respect to your labels and stories, as if you were looking at mountains from the sky. We asked you to notice what it's like to create space between you and your labels: to venture beyond your labels and stories. If not labels, what will you orient to instead? We offer an answer to this question in the next chapter, where we explore the idea of values.

CHAPTER 6

Identifying What Truly Matters

When was the last time you felt good about your life? Maybe you had the thought, "Wow, this is really nice." It could've been a moment when you were effortlessly present and at peace, when the mind chatter was quiet, or when your defenses were completely down. Some might describe this as a "flow state." You might have wished you could have more moments just like that. Go back in time as far as you need to find that moment. If you can't recall one, use your imagination. Picture a scene where this could happen and immerse yourself in it.

. . .

. . .

. . .

This "flow" moment tells you something about your *values*—what truly matters to you. How often do you have these moments of pure inner contentment? If you're deep in the struggle with perfectionism, we're guessing not often. More likely, you're so focused on working harder, chasing accomplishments, checking items off your to-do list, and not messing up that you neglect your values. You may also have moments that *should* feel fulfilling because they're in line with your values (another rule) but actually don't, like going on a hike with your family and still feeling empty afterward. The result of not knowing, pursuing, or connecting with your values is existential anxiety and dread—as if you're perpetually waiting for something, not realizing that the waiting has become your life.

Clarifying Values

By "values," we mean something different from how most people define them. Values are (1) freely chosen and intrinsically meaningful (you'd care about them even if no one knew you did); (2) directions, not destinations (you can *always* move toward your values and they can never be completed); and (3) entirely within your control (you don't rely on external factors to enact them). The primary function of values is to provide guidance when you're lost, like a lighthouse amid choppy seas.

Knowing your values is important, because we're going to ask you to use your values to evaluate the quality of your life: a "good" life means you're living consistently with your values, and a "good" action is one that moves you toward your values. This is different from judging your actions based on how they make you feel; in that case, a "good" move is one that decreases or regulates an unpleasant thought or emotion. The distinction matters because you have much more control over whether you meet the values criterion for "good" than the feelings criterion for "good." Using the values criterion is saying yes to someone to help them, whereas using the feelings criterion is saying yes to avoid feeling guilty.

Values are *not* imposed by real or perceived expectations from your environment (for example, success), readily checked off a list (like going to church on Sunday), or outside your control (such as being loved). The condition that a value must be within your control can be confusing because you might intrinsically value being loved and you can always be loved more, satisfying the first two criteria. However, being loved doesn't count as a value if you can't make it happen. While you can choose to act lovingly, you cannot choose to be loved. The "within your control" imperative is tied to the idea that living according to your values determines the goodness of your life. If you choose values over which you have no control, you inadvertently relinquish the power to make your life "good." Consequently, you'll end up feeling helpless, similar to if you let feelings and rules choose your behaviors for you.

Values can be *anything*. Examples include advocacy, authenticity, autonomy, compassion, creativity, connection, integrity, reliability, and nature. Reflect on what makes you glad to be alive, excited to start each day, or willing to make space for pain—start from there. There are no good or bad, right or wrong values. Your values are right because you choose them; no justification is needed. Resist looking to others to identify your values for you, because the only person who will enjoy a life filled with meaning or who will ultimately suffer from living a life disconnected from values is you. Certainly, your values may be influenced by and even overlap with those around you. However, at the end of the day, they are yours to live.

The Function of Values

Besides serving as your lighthouse, values color trying moments with purpose. They're the reason you would choose to go camping in a bug-infested forest when you could be at home in your warm bed. Values give meaning to listening to a friend complain about the same problem for the twenty-seventh time, waking up at 4:00 a.m. for a sunrise hike, and cleaning up dog vomit from the couch. For instance, giving up a day of skiing to spend time with your sick partner probably isn't fun. Nonetheless, you might *choose* to do that if you connect with your value of showing up for others in times of need. As you pick up mucus-filled tissue off the floor, you might see that every move you've made that day toward "being there for your partner" over carving the slopes is you being exactly the person you want to be, even if it's the less enjoyable option. Conversely, picture yourself doing the exact same thing without connecting with your value of showing up. Perhaps you felt obligated to do it or subtly pressured by your partner. Your day might look exactly the same, yet your internal landscape would be vastly different.

By giving meaning to our actions, values can make us choose to approach things we typically—or even instinctively—avoid. For example, people generally don't yearn for muscle soreness. However, if we associate muscle aches with gains in strength (assuming being strong is a value), we might even want to feel sore after a rigorous workout. In this frame of reference, being sore *means* you're getting stronger, so you'd now choose to approach this uncomfortable feeling. For a more macabre example, consider how willing you'd be to give up one of your thumbs. Probably not very. Now, what if giving up your thumb would save your loved one from a creepy murderer who accepts only thumbs for ransom? If your answer isn't an immediate "of course," we're guessing you're at least willing to consider giving up your thumb in this hypothetical scenario since it now *means* saving your loved one.

On the flip side, life without values is excruciating. Without values, you'd be going through the motions, schlepping through a never-ending to-do list, and counting down the minutes at the end of every workday, all while trying to convince yourself that what you're doing is what you want to do. Being disconnected from values deprives you of the ability to appreciate life—even when you're doing things that *should* make life worth living. People who have interesting jobs, enough money to live comfortably, a loving family, amazing friends, and cool hobbies can still feel empty. This pain can then turn into suffering when they admonish themselves for not feeling happy despite all their privileges. Being in a situation that *should* make you happy doesn't guarantee you'll feel happy because emotions don't follow logic. That's just how it goes. However, if you pause for a second and acknowledge—really, properly acknowledge—how your actions are contributing to the life you want and the legacy you hope to leave behind, it's much easier to find meaning in and motivation for your actions.

Identifying Your Values

Your values represent who you want to be and what you want to stand for. Rather than "be yourself," the advice with values is, "be who you *care* to be." Be the person you'd respect. Be the person who'll look back on their life and be proud of what they've done (and not done). Be the person fear says you can't be.

Identifying values is especially tricky if you're still attached to notions of how things should be or who you should be, because "shoulds" and "values" get blurred. Do you value success, or do you believe you "should" strive for success? Do you value being able to provide for your family, or do you believe that's the "right" thing to do? The issue with "should values" is that they don't provide you with the same drive that freely chosen values do. Instead, they only lead to more waiting and dissatisfaction.

To identify your true values, create space from rules, make room for the discomfort of being wrong, and simply observe the pain of the discrepancy between your current actions and the life you want to have. Take a few intentional breaths. When all is said and done, what do you want to be about? What do you want to stand for? What will make pain worth experiencing?

Here are more questions you can use to clarify your values:

1. What would you value or work toward even if no one knew about it?

2. If you didn't have to worry about any repercussions, what would you do with your life?

3. If you won the lottery, what would you do?

4. What do you want your epitaph to say?

5. What do you want your loved ones to remember about you after you die?

6. What brings you joy—no matter how small?

7. What would you choose to do again and again, even knowing with hindsight all the pain it would bring?

Ponder these questions and write down words or phrases that capture your values in your notebook.

This exercise can bring you closer to identifying your values, but there's no sure way to be correct. Values are not about finding the right answer or right motivation (rules again); they're about discovering what feeds your soul and warms your heart. We can get closer and closer to understanding what they are, but our inherent complexity as humans makes it impossible to nail our values perfectly. Our needs are always changing, and the ways in which we can meet them are infinite. (Sit with that uncertainty for a moment.)

Continue refining the values you listed in your notebook over the next week. Make them more specific. For instance, instead of the general "relationships," pare that down to the more targeted "being a caring partner" or "being present with my family." Take time to flesh out your list so that you're clear on what each value means to you.

Then act on your values and track the effects of doing so. Do you like your life more than before? When we say "like," we don't mean having more fun; we mean finding difficult times worth going through, being proud of how you spent your time, and discerning meaning in your actions. If little has changed, reevaluate your list of values. Find ones that work for you.

Connecting with Your Values

Identifying values is only part of the work. Another part is connecting with your values, which means realizing the purpose behind your actions in the moment and seeing those actions as steps toward something bigger than your current situation. This is different from "having a positive attitude" by retroactively telling yourself you really do care about picking up the slack in your group projects because you "value" being a responsible team member. You've probably already tried that, and you're too smart to convince yourself of something you don't believe anyway. Connecting with values is about finding meaning that actually exists.

Values are *actively* enacted. They don't happen to you; you act on them of your own volition. For example, for me, Clarissa, meticulously checking survey setups and entering data for research is pure drudgery. Yet reflecting on how these tasks contribute to my value of generating and communicating useful knowledge that may help someone at some point makes me *choose* to do them—even when I can choose otherwise. In fact, we almost always have the option to choose otherwise; we rarely *have to* do anything (that's rules at work). I don't *have to* apply for jobs after graduating. I don't *have to* be nice to everyone. You don't *have to* help your children with their homework. You don't *have to* get to the airport four hours before your flight departure time. You don't *have to* do your laundry every Sunday. Even if you don't consciously recognize it, you're *choosing* to do these things.

Choosing in this context is about your willingness (or unwillingness) to take on the consequences of your actions. When you say you "have to" do something, it's probably more that you're unwilling to bear the consequences of not doing it, like how someone may be unwilling to drop out of graduate school in their sixth year and have their efforts come to naught or to risk the ire of their partner by bailing on movie night. As much as a choice is disagreeable given your circumstances and values, it's still a choice. At least, framing your actions in this way provides an alternative perspective. I *choose to* apply for jobs after graduating. I *choose to* be nice to everyone. You *choose to* help your children with their homework. You *choose to* get to the airport four hours before your flight departure time. You *choose to* do your laundry every Sunday. If you perceive these actions as choices you make, the option to choose differently becomes obvious: just as you can *choose to* wait until you feel motivated before starting a new project, you can also *choose to* start a project even when you don't feel motivated. Envision what your life would look like if you made choices based on your values rather than on rules and threats.

Following your values not only releases you from perfectionism by offering a new direction, but it also gives you a sense of fulfillment and vitality. At the same time, your mind is going to generate all sorts of reasons for staying exactly where you are. Whenever you notice tension between perfectionistic rules and your values, ask yourself: Is it more important to be right or to be free? Taking that first step toward your values means letting go of the structures that have been regulating your actions ever since you could remember—and that's terrifying. But like a child who is empowered by their ability to walk and venture outside, you might find that this fear is eclipsed by all the world has to offer.

Troubleshooting Values

Values aren't always a walk in the park. Many people assume that it "should" be easy to know what's important to them and that when they know what matters, they "should" be able to "just do it." You might believe some version of that yourself. Coherence says that if you care enough about something, you'll do it. Conversely, if you don't do something, it means you don't care enough about it. When you get ensnared in these cognitive processes, pursuing values becomes more complicated. You may fixate on finding the "right" values, procrastinate your values, treat values like rules, or drift from your values. It's helpful to understand the challenges you may face as you identify and connect with your values so you'll know what to do if they happen.

Identifying the wrong values. Values are wonderful when we know what they are, but that's not always the case. For example, your perfectionistic mind might be wondering if you've written down the right values. After all, identifying values is high stakes. If you select the wrong values and work toward those, your life will be incongruent with your true values. You will have massively screwed up.

Take a mental step back and take stock of what's happening inside your head right now. Is this another round of Perfectionism Says? The rule might be, "You need to identify the correct values so you can live a valued life." Rules can be tricky to spot when your mind gets noisy, so float above the chatter. Watch the arguing and rationalizing. Get in touch with the part of you that is free from rules, expectations, anxiety, stress, and worry. Be willing to be wrong when you state your values.

Being unprepared to act on values. As you embark on your chosen values, your mind might give you another rule about needing to "be ready" before you act on them. Readiness can mean different things, but it primarily entails taking care of everything else besides values. For example, you need to be on top of taking care of your children and keeping up with basic chores before you start exercising, or you need to get rid of your commitment anxiety before you start dating. Your mind promises that you'll eventually get to your values *after* you've gotten your life in order, so you toil away for years to prepare yourself for the life you really want, effectively procrastinating your values.

How much longer are you going to wait for your mind to give you the green light? Going through life waiting for it to become meaningful is depressing. Instead, relax perfectionistic standards to pursue your values: organize game night with your friends even if that means rushing an assignment, play the new song you learned for your family even if you haven't practiced it fully, or take a poetry class even if you've never read a poem before. When it comes down to it, will you pick perfection or purpose?

Choosing among "conflicting" values. As you start following multiple values, you'll probably run into the problem of values that appear to conflict with one another. If you value family *and* your work ethic, is the values-consistent move to take time off work for a family trip to Yosemite or to postpone the trip to complete your current projects? Sometimes, one value clearly outweighs the other. If the family trip is specifically scheduled to celebrate your child's thirteenth birthday, then you'll likely decide to take time off work. But let's say you don't get the luxury of an easy out. How do you choose among values when they're pulling you in different directions?

Part of this predicament comes down to rules again, particularly those around knowing the right answer: "I need to make the right decision," "I can't fail at my values," or "I need to know the correct value before acting." Perfectionism wants you to use logic to figure out your life before you live it, but logic can't do that for you. By now, you know what to do. Be bold and choose anyway. Be open to uncertainty. (Seeking certainty is the coherence trap at work.) Learn from your lived experience and trust that your cumulative experiences will guide you to where you need to be.

In navigating ostensibly conflicting values, it may also be helpful to remember that while values are relatively stable, the ways you choose to enact them are more flexible. If you value caring for the environment, you could go all out and stop purchasing plastic items, driving a car, using air-conditioning, and eating meat—among uncountable other things. However, that's unsustainable. Instead, you can act on your environment value by biking, eating a mostly plant-based diet, and recycling. That leaves room for you to do other things you care about, like going camping and reading feminist literature.

The reality is that you have limited time, energy, and resources. You can't follow your values in all situations all the time, so you'll have to constantly grapple with the dilemma of prioritizing different values in different contexts. In this sense, values don't come for free. You inevitably have to give up something you value to attain something else you value. The crux is: After you decide how to allocate your time, can you sit with the discomfort that comes with knowing you're missing out on other values?

Veering away from your values. Staying connected with your values as you move through life is an ongoing process. Your mind may succeed at distracting you from your values more than you'd prefer. Your values may change as you grow older. As you test out your values, the picture will become clearer and you can adjust your actions accordingly. Maybe you don't really care about being nice, and as uncomfortable as it makes you, being assertive gives you a sense of doing right by yourself. Maybe you don't actually value working for a prestigious company and find more meaning in doing freelance work.

One way to stay true to your values is using your lived experience to reflect on whether your values are working for you. Remember, feelings provide useful information, so use them as data. Living in line with your values feels qualitatively different from going through the motions and following shoulds. You can't predict exactly how you'll feel (you might even still feel uncomfortable), but following your values means you'd choose the same behaviors even if you could start over. For instance, you may feel bored helping your child with their algebra homework, especially when you could be rewatching *Rick and Morty*. However, given the chance to choose again, you'd still select the path that contains more unpleasant feelings because it's the one that gets you closer to the parent you want to be. That's the power of values.

✹   ✹   ✹

Values are freely chosen, personally meaningful qualities or ways of being you can use to guide your behaviors, like challenge, courage, and humility. They give your actions meaning by linking them to a bigger purpose, so that walking your dog is not just a chore, but also a way for you to show that you care. To identify your values, get in touch with the part of you that transcends rules and fears. In this space, ask yourself what you care about. What would you say if you didn't have to be accountable to anyone but yourself ten years from now?

Once you've identified your values, act on them. Make room for uncertainty as you enact your values. You won't always know if your values are correct before acting. If your values aren't serving you, revise them. Use your experience of trying out values to inform your selections; clarifying values may require trial and error.

The beautiful thing about values is that they're omnipresent. The opportunity to orient yourself toward values exists in every moment. Values are not future consequences; they are—in fact, they can only be—experienced in the here and now. In the next chapter, we discuss how to keep your attention focused on the present even when your mind and society insist you evaluate your life in terms of outcomes.

CHAPTER 7

Focusing on Process over Outcome

What are you proudest of in your life? Take a moment to think about that.

...

...

...

Was your answer some sort of accomplishment? For example, graduating, having children, buying a house, or getting a prestigious job? If so, that's unsurprising. We're primed to define success in terms of outcomes, because those are what society values. Nobody gets a prize for work ethic—only profits earned, assets acquired, and other tangible products.

How about what you're most ashamed of? Society also tells us what we should feel embarrassed about or ashamed of: dropping out of school, being unmarried, earning less than a certain threshold, struggling with psychological symptoms, and even idealistically pursuing our goals. We intuitively know these associations (rich = good, depressed = bad) from the cultural messages we implicitly and explicitly receive, like ads showing that people who take psychotropic drugs are happier than those who don't. Understandably, that leaves us persistently wanting (at least) one of two things: (1) bigger and better accomplishments (more "good" outcomes) or (2) avoidance of mistakes at all costs (fewer "bad" outcomes).

The issue with focusing exclusively on outcomes—on "good" or "bad"—is that you lose sight of the process. But the "how" matters because you have more control over *how* you do things than *what* you get from doing them or what ultimately happens because of them. For instance, it's easier to focus on connecting with nature during a hike than to complete the hike within two hours, because there are almost always variables outside your control that affect outcomes. You could twist your ankle. A storm could roll in. You could encounter a mountain lion. It's outside your power to guarantee certain outcomes, just like the Cavaliers can have LeBron James on their team and still lose in the NBA finals.

Moreover, obsessing over outcomes at the expense of process means you're letting the present slip through your fingers. You reminisce over old accomplishments, dwell on past failures, and worry about the future. Meanwhile, the present space you actually occupy is ignored. If focusing on outcomes helped you find contentment, all would be peachy. But be honest: Has life been more meaningful when you've focused on the process or the outcome?

The Opportunity Cost of Attention

Process versus outcome is a matter of attention or orientation. In other words, the distinction is *where* you direct your attention. If you had unlimited attention, you could focus on everything without missing out on anything, such that you could fuss over sloppy table setting while still being fully present for your granddaughter's wedding.

Alas, humans have a finite attention span, which means every time you give your attention to something, you inadvertently take it away from something else. Imagine you're playing with your child, nibling (gender-neutral term for niece or nephew), or grandchild. You could be arranging blocks with them, teaching them how to walk, or playing peekaboo. Suddenly, your mind reminds you that you still haven't RSVPed to Eric and Becky's party, and your attention leaps from playing to problem solving. You pick up your phone and text Eric, leaving little Burrhus alone with his blocks.

Looking at this situation, can you see some benefit to being continuously present with Burrhus and dealing with life tasks later? Perhaps you'll catch an inscrutable facial expression you haven't observed before or you'll hear him say your name for the first time. Beyond that, you're wholly embracing the experience of being with Burrhus as he grows up. You're also establishing being present as a habit, which can be applied in other situations, like when you want to concentrate on a recipe or listen to your partner talk about their day.

To be sure, "missing out" occurs only when you care about the ongoing activity. You don't "miss out" on boring conversations with strangers or pointless meetings. You can afford to miss out on certain things but not others, like opening presents on Christmas morning, watching your children get taller and more agile, supporting a friend through a messy breakup, and witnessing your favorite sports team make history.

Managing your attention is about *intentionally choosing* what to focus on versus miss out on. What things are you glad to let go of, and what things do you wish to be present for? Like it or not, you're going to miss out on so many things. Not all of us are going to visit the Louvre, hold a starfish, eat elk's heart, climb a fourteener, or grow our own produce. Given that you have only so much attentional energy, prioritize where you want to spend it. Do you want to expend precious energy on mistakes you've made, awkward conversations you can't redo, and worst-case scenarios, or on your anniversary dinner, your toddler's first steps, and your dog wearing booties for the first time?

Do a quick self-assessment. In your notebook, tally up the percentage of attention you've spent on your values in the past week. What did you get? Does that number reflect where you want to be?

Attending Is a Skill

If you'd like to change this number, practice attending. Attending is a skill. With practice, you can increase the control you have over the target of your attention. This means you'll be able to *choose* between deliberating on missteps at work or concentrating on beating your roommates at Catan, worrying about whether your neighbors like you or being engrossed in the action sequences of *John Wick*, and stressing over what to have for lunch or relishing the warmth of a hug.

Think of attention as a spotlight on your mind's stage. At any point, you have various actors milling about. Some of them are loud and obnoxious, clearly vying for the spotlight, while others are happy to blend into the background and be ignored. You may be tempted to play the role of director, trying to get actors to say their lines differently or move more forcefully, but they're terrible at following instructions. In fact, the more you try to direct them, the more unruly they get. So give up directing. Instead, take control of the spotlight. Even if you can't control who's onstage and what they're doing, you can choose who gets your attention and who remains in the shadows.

This may be frustrating to hear. More than anything, we'd love to teach you how to get rid of all the mediocre actors or at least train them to be more competent. We agree that it'd be much nicer if you could manage exactly what happens onstage. Yet we're asking you to leave the mediocre actors alone, to find a way to focus on the helpful ones *without* first nudging the unhelpful ones offstage. If you remember some of the content of chapters 3 and 4, you may recognize that we're asking you to do this out of pragmatism. We're asking you to move the spotlight, not the actors, because you can move the actors only so much. They're stubborn folks who do as they please. You may also remember that the actors are thoughts and feelings that don't inherently have the power to push you around or ruin your life. Like tiny pebbles in your shoe, the actors may be annoying and you may prefer to toss them out. Nonetheless, you can move toward your goals and values in their presence.

To provide some context, think of a breathing meditation—it most closely resembles how to manage attention in the way we're describing. A breathing meditation typically involves bringing your awareness to your breath—each inhale, each exhale—noticing when your mind wanders, and gently returning your awareness to breathing when it does. Sometimes, people fail to keep their attention on their breath and conclude they didn't do the exercise correctly. However, the target skill is less about staying focused on breathing and more about *redirecting* your awareness to breathing when it inevitably drifts. Thus, the more times you catch your mind wandering and bring your attention back to breathing, the stronger you get at shifting your attention. Remember, it's the process, not the outcome.

The ability to redirect your awareness and attention is especially crucial when it comes to worry, which is a marquee feature in perfectionism and can feel all-consuming. Reflect on what it's like to be stuck in a worry spiral, with what-ifs followed by more what-ifs and relentless images of disasters to come. When you get trapped in a worry spiral, it's hard to disentangle yourself if you (a) don't notice that you're in a worry spiral in the first place and (b) don't know what to do even when you do notice you're worrying.

Being intentional with attention helps with both aspects. It trains you to see the worry spiral as *another* actor on your mind's stage, one who is gleefully hogging the spotlight and insisting that you listen to their uninterrupted monologue. When you take this perspective, it becomes obvious that the worry spiral is not special. It may be louder and more desperate than other voices, but it doesn't have special stage privileges. Moreover, directing your attention in this manner makes other options salient to you, because it allows you to see *everything* onstage. You'll see not only worry, but also your friend's opinion on oat versus soy milk, the cool breeze on your face, and the merry melody of a yellow warbler. When you function at this level of awareness, you can more easily extract yourself from worrying and catastrophizing. It just takes practice to get there.

How to Redirect Attention

Thankfully, practicing redirecting your attention is convenient in the sense that you can do it anywhere and anytime. The present is always here for you. Try it now (read along with us below or follow the audio recording of this "Taking Control of Your Mind's Spotlight" exercise, available at http://www.newharbinger.com/48459).

Take a step back from the hustle and bustle of your mind. Go to the theater balcony and watch the actors onstage, jostling with one another. Notice the cacophony as they talk simultaneously. Notice the set décor. Notice the material of the seats and the layout of the theater. Now look outside the theater. What is happening right now? What do you hear, smell, see, touch, even taste? Get in touch with each of those senses. Really, do it.

. . .

. . .

. . .

Listen to what your senses are telling you about your environment. What are the sounds? What does it feel like to be sitting where you are? Attend to each stimulus *as it enters your awareness*. Keep doing that. Pretend you're following along with a metronome of the present. With every tick, you're being present.

If your mind wanders, great. This is your chance to practice bringing your attention back to the now, which may be challenging initially. Be patient. Allow yourself to be imperfect at this. Start by looking at the place to which your mind wandered. Maybe even notice the feeling of stuckness to this place. Now look at all the actors onstage competing for the spotlight. Once you have them in your mind's eye, nudge your spotlight to the sounds, smells, and sights of the present. Maybe you did it for a second. That counts. The idea is to keep practicing exerting control over your attention so that the next time a worry spiral sucks you in or stress sends you bouncing off the walls, you can get out of the crevice, expand your awareness, and choose where you want to be in the wider landscape.

Why do we ask you to do this? One of the actors might be complaining that this exercise is a waste of time. They're saying that you could've sent at least four emails in the time that you took to survey your mind's stage. Perfectionism despises idleness, after all. Except you're not being idle, not even close. How much effort does it take you to pull back from your anxiety, stress, and worry and redirect your attention to something more relevant to your current needs? How difficult is it to get unstuck from the black hole of what-ifs and shoulds and orient to the present moment? How impossible does it feel to resist distraction from social media exactly when you need to muster all of your concentration?

What you're doing *is* work. You're working to maneuver your rusty spotlight, which carries the inertia of years of ruminating and worrying. The work is actively and intentionally choosing the input for your life going forward. You can choose to feed your mind with stale thoughts or with fresh insights. Consider what a new attentional diet could do for you. How much could you gain from the power of being mindful?

Awareness of Awareness (or Meta-Awareness)

There's another layer to attending: awareness of awareness, or being aware that you're aware. Think of your mind like a matryoshka doll (nesting doll), with dolls upon dolls of awareness. We introduced a closely related skill in chapter 3: namely, watching the process of thinking—realizing you *are thinking*—instead of automatically believing thoughts, like recognizing that you're surrounded by air molecules instead of empty space.

Catching when your attention has wandered or gotten sucked into a worry spiral is by definition tricky because you've lost awareness of your awareness. What you're aiming to regain sometimes is this meta-awareness, to see that your awareness has wandered off. In a sense, because you can't always be aware of being aware (or, at least, it may not be worth the effort), what you're practicing is decreasing those moments of rumination, worry, and being on autopilot—when you get so caught up in your thoughts and feelings that you become completely disconnected from the here and now and don't even realize it.

As humans, we're bound to get distracted uncountable times throughout our lives. In fact, obsessively holding on to the spotlight can present its own set of problems; it's probably emotionally and cognitively taxing to be constantly redirecting your attention. Moreover, it's sometimes healthy to let your mind wander and go on autopilot. But we want you to decide when that happens. The more you practice being aware of not being aware, the easier it will be to notice when your attention goes off-leash.

Once you improve your meta-awareness, the next part is bringing your attention to the here and now (or wherever makes sense for you). Being aware of awareness means you can see yourself falling through the rabbit hole. To get out of it, first take a mental step backward. Look at the rabbit hole itself, the thoughts and feelings you're having—be they anxiety, stress, worry, loneliness, shame, or guilt. See if you can observe what the thoughts and feelings are doing or how they are moving (refer to the "Acknowledging Without Surrendering" section in chapter 3 for more details).

This mental step backward is akin to zooming out of a picture. An image may seem almost claustrophobic up close (just look up microscopic images of a spider's face or paper), but when you create space from it, you have more room to operate. For example, if you're chatting with a friend and your mind begins rattling off your to-do list, practice pausing, stepping back, and looking at the bigger picture. At first, you may still see the worry spiral—your thoughts nervously pacing back and forth, theatrically narrating the worst-case scenarios about to befall you. But as you continue to zoom out, other objects come into view: the words your friend is saying, the theme of the conversation you're having, your friend, your friendship, the reasons you care about this friend. The spotlight is in your hands. Grab the reins of your attention and be intentional with it.

Clarifying Mindfulness

Attending is part of *mindfulness*, which has multiple definitions in popular culture. For example, the words "mindfulness" and "meditation" are sometimes used synonymously, so people often think of them as the same thing. Others think of the soothing voice of a yoga instructor bowing to the light inside each and every one of us or guided meditation tracks with ambient background sounds. These can certainly be a part of mindfulness, but the broader idea of mindfulness is about *intentionality*—actively choosing where you focus your energy. Perhaps a better term for what we're talking about is "being mindful." Hence, mindfulness goes beyond sitting on the floor and regulating your breath for thirty minutes. It's focusing on reading articles instead of being distracted by text notifications; it's appreciating the instruments backing a song instead of treating music as white noise; it's feeling the sun's warmth as you recline on a picnic blanket instead of fretting over how much you're perspiring. As long as you're deliberately choosing to give your attention to these stimuli, you're being mindful.

You may also hear people talk about being present rather than being mindful. The reason for the emphasis on being present is that most of us are bad at it. We're pretty good at ruminating on the past ("I shouldn't have made that stupid mistake") and worrying about the future ("What if I never achieve my goals?"). But what tends to be most difficult in being mindful is the being present part, which is why it's the skill that will produce the most gains. For instance, if you're already excellent at the front crawl and backstroke, practicing the butterfly is the most efficient way to become a better swimmer (rather than trying to go from a nine to a ten on the other strokes). However, that doesn't mean the front crawl and backstroke are rendered irrelevant. It just means you're adding another arrow to your quiver, giving you a broader range of response options from which to choose depending on the situation. Another reason for homing in on the present moment is that living happens only in the here and now. Each moment you spend in the past or the future is a moment lost to living *now*.

Choosing Process over Outcome

Developing the ability to choose the here and now *when it serves you* makes it easier to prioritize process over outcome. This is the skill of shifting your focus from "Did I get what I wanted?" to "Did I do it how I wanted?" Sure, society doesn't care as much about how you get things done; it cares more that you do. But as much as society has conditioned you to define success in terms of outcomes, you still get to choose what to strive for in life. You have the power to redefine success in terms of process, and wrangling your attention effectively gives you the ability to pivot toward process despite the allure of outcomes.

Recall the last time you were aiming for a specific outcome: a positive performance evaluation, approval from your peers, a clean home, baking a perfectly moist cake, or making the right purchase. Rather than focusing on the prize, imagine if you had chosen the here and now and attended to your values in the moment. For example, instead of worrying about what your boss and coworkers thought of you every time you spoke up in a meeting, you connected with your values of learning and collaboration as you shared your perspective. Instead of worrying about whether your date liked you, you connected with your value of being open to new people and let curiosity guide your behavior. This is choosing process over outcome. Examine the role's of process and outcome in your life. In your notebook, write down two to three examples from your life contrasting process against outcome. Which side is more fulfilling?

As you've been reading this chapter, you might have experienced some resistance to our recommendation to orient toward process. That's expected. Moving away from outcomes is unnerving. Your mind may be yelling all sorts of things at you. You may worry about losing motivation to excel or falling behind others who are still outcome-oriented. Rules and self-labels may be getting activated. "I *should* always try to be the best." "I've *always been good at going after my goals*." Great. Notice all of that. This is the spiral. Take a step back and look at it as it churns. Now look outside the spiral. What else is happening on your mind's stage? What are your values saying?

We care about process, because choosing it liberates us from the perceived need to control outcomes that are fundamentally outside our control. You can't make people happy, but you can treat them with love and empathy. You can't force your children to be well behaved (especially in public spaces), but you can treat them with patience. You can't guarantee a stress-free holiday, but you can give yourself a break when things go awry. Take the burden of being responsible for outcomes off your shoulders. Ultimately, do you want your epitaph to say that you started a company, made millions of dollars, got two PhDs, and traveled to forty-three counties or that you were kind, generous, accepting, and brave?

* * *

Focusing on the outcome of your efforts over the process of working toward a goal can make you feel like you're constantly chasing something and can entrench your attention in the past or the future, omitting the present from your purview. However, the present is the only space in which life occurs. Moreover, because your attention is finite, spending attention on anxiety, stress, and worry means you are potentially missing out on things more worthy of your attention, like the people and activities you love.

Although you can't control whether and which thoughts and feelings show up to grab your attention, you *can* control how much attention to give them. This is the idea of being mindful, which essentially is about being intentional with your attention. One way to practice being mindful is by deliberately directing your attention as if it were a spotlight on a stage. Take stock of the actors on the stage and choose which ones are worth your attention, given your goals and values. If you notice the spotlight getting stuck on certain actors (like when you go down a worry spiral), zoom out and reorient to the whole stage. Then choose (again) to whom you want to give your attention. Being mindful is bringing yourself back to the stage and its actors again, and again, and again.

One thing that *is* worth your attention is yourself—or, more specifically, your health and wellness. In the next chapter, we describe why we think self-care and self-kindness matter, even if perfectionism vehemently disagrees.

CHAPTER 8

Being Kind to Yourself

What comes to mind when you hear the word "self-compassion"? Brunch with mimosas? A warm bath with perfumed soaps? Time to eat lunch on a busy day? A backpacking trip in the Moab desert? Like many terms in psychology, "self-compassion" has taken on various meanings to the point where it's become somewhat of an empty placeholder. Is self-compassion spending five hundred dollars on a spa package or telling yourself you're beautiful every morning when you look in the mirror? Given the careless marketing of self-compassion, it's no wonder so many of us reject it.

You may be one of those people who say, "I don't have time to sit down for ten minutes just to breathe. I can breathe while I get stuff done." For the record, we also reject the mainstream conceptualization of self-compassion as an infrequent luxury or tangible product. Rather, we see self-compassion as *acts* of self-kindness or self-gentleness; it's treating yourself like any reasonable person would or like you would treat someone who deserves to be treated well. Given the multiple connotations of "self-compassion," we're going to use "self-kindness" instead, to sidestep any pointless tug-of-war with your mind.

Clarifying Self-Kindness

Self-kindness is a category of behaviors that function to preserve, protect, or enhance well-being. It is not self-indulgence (as so beautifully expressed by Audre Lorde in her essay collection A *Burst of Light*: "Caring for myself is not self-indulgence, it is self-preservation, and that is an act of political warfare"). It is not gratuitous or optional. At its core, self-kindness is about keeping your body well through sleep, diet, and exercise; your brain sharp through curiosity and stimulation; and your heart pulsing through social connections and self-respecting boundaries. It is essential to your quality of life.

Because self-kindness is bound by function or the purpose an action serves (like perfectionism), anything can count as self-kindness as long as it's about taking care of yourself. Self-kindness ranges from grand gestures, like buying a new laptop, to oft-overlooked actions, like saying no to a task to which you feel obligated to say yes. For some people, taking a break from work and watching *Broadchurch* is an act of self-kindness, whereas for others, it's not starting another episode at midnight when you have an 8:00 meeting the next morning. Whether an action is self-kind depends on *why* you are doing the behavior. Is it to avoid discomfort or to improve quality of life?

A lot of the time with perfectionism, self-kindness is simply giving yourself permission to make mistakes—to be human. If you've spent hours agonizing over how to start an email to your boss, self-kindness is picking one option and sending the email anyway. In doing so, you're basically saying to yourself, "It's okay if I use the wrong salutation. I'm acceptable regardless of how this person receives my email." If you exercise some perspective taking, preventing yourself from sending the email is equivalent to forcing someone to sit in front of their computer screen for hours exploring every single possible reaction to every permutation of greeting until they know exactly what the right answer is. (And even then, they won't.) If you find yourself arguing with this logic, ask yourself, "Would I ask someone I care about to go through that amount of stress to please their boss?"

Self-kindness is an everyday activity. Many people have the impression that they can make up for consistently running themselves into the ground if they intermittently go all out on self-care, sort of like doing a juice cleanse to reset the system. Accordingly, they focus on the grand-gesture end of the spectrum, raising the barrier to engaging in self-kindness and making themselves more likely to avoid it. This is like setting an exercise minimum of three-hundred push-ups—in that case, you'd probably try to get out of exercising however you could.

In reality, "smaller" acts may be more significant precisely because they can be completed more easily and frequently. This point becomes clearer with an analogy. If you think of self-kindness like other healthy lifestyle habits—such as dental hygiene—it would be odd to assert that you can safely skip daily teeth brushing because you go for annual dental cleanings. What about all the time in between? Germs, plaque, and bacteria are constantly accumulating, and allowing them to linger unchecked increases your risk of illness and disease. You don't wait until you get cavities to start brushing your teeth regularly, so why would you wait for torturous "breakdowns" to start taking care of your mental and emotional health? In fact, the *absence* of cavities tells you that regular brushing is working. Similarly, self-kindness is best practiced as a habit. It's easier to make up for the occasional late night than consecutive sleepless nights; it's unreasonable to expect yourself to be adequately rejuvenated after sleeping in one morning if you've been constantly sleep-deprived. More generally, it's absurd to expect infrequent injections of self-kindness to do the colossal job of neutralizing your burnout and quieting relentless self-criticism.

Continuing the analogy: neither do you brush your teeth only when you feel like it or when you have time to do it. You understand the necessity of the task, so you make it happen. Yet you likely denounce self-kindness as superfluous, a luxury you can't afford and don't need. You prioritize everything above taking care of yourself and wonder why you fall asleep at meetings, make careless mistakes at work, forget to reply to texts, and zone out during important conversations. That's problematic.

Instead, like brushing your teeth, practice self-kindness as a matter of *choice*, which means being kind to yourself regardless of your mood, motivation, or schedule—make self-kindness unconditional. You may even feel annoyed doing it in the moment, just as you may be loath to brush your teeth after a long night out as your eyes struggle to stay open. But the whole point is that you don't brush your teeth to make yourself feel good. You do it *for your own good*. Conversely, you can choose not to brush your teeth for a multitude of reasons. Perhaps your tiredness outweighs your need for cleanliness. That's fine too. What matters is that you're the one choosing in light of all the relevant information.

Barriers to Self-Kindness

Although we've likened self-kindness to dental hygiene, it's just as simple as and more complicated than that. It's simple in the sense that you roughly know what actions are healthy and how to do them. For example, you probably already know to put away blue light–emitting devices close to bedtime, eat a balanced diet, exercise regularly, and seek friendship. Even if you didn't know these things, you know, at the very least, that it's detrimental to your well-being to argue with your partner over not putting away dishes according to your maximally efficient system, replaying conversations with friends and analyzing them for potential offenses, and missing sleep to meet deadlines.

Nonetheless, there's more to self-kindness than doing the obvious things. If not, we'd all already be amazing at it. It's more complicated in the sense that self-kindness builds on all the skills we've discussed already: you need to detach from the noise and stress and connect with your heart.

A major barrier to self-kindness is believing you don't deserve it. You buy into the false narrative that self-kindness is a treat, something you get to partake in only when you've *earned* it. Imagine that: needing to do something special to *earn* your toothbrushing. If you know anything about perfectionism, you also know that you'll never do enough—and, deep down, you'll never *be* enough—to deserve self-kindness. No breaks until you get everything on your to-do list done. No love for the "unlikable loser." No compliments when you're "fundamentally flawed." The very self-criticism for which self-kindness is an antidote keeps you from giving and receiving self-kindness. Thus, self-kindness has several prerequisites: observing the stream of self-critical thoughts without getting swept up in them (refer back to chapter 3), creating space for the discomfort of feeling undeserving (see chapter 4), and separating the self from unhelpful labels (see chapter 5).

You may also be afraid of being nice to yourself because of what that might unleash. That sounds counterintuitive, but in essence, what we're positing is that part of the resistance to self-kindness is a fear of removing the weight you've been using to keep yourself down—almost like you're afraid of the consequences of being able to do whatever you want. What do you anticipate would happen if you were to accept praise and renounce the "not good enough" narrative? Perhaps your mind reasons that you'd fall into ruin. You'd be worse off than you already are. You'd achieve less and procrastinate more because you're "lazy" and "stupid." As we discussed in chapter 5, even if that were the case, there would still be plenty of reason to be wary about using self-criticism as fuel. For one, it creates tremendous unnecessary suffering. Two, the stick approach doesn't work in the long term. You become resentful and you burn out, making the criticism a self-fulfilling prophecy.

A deeper part of the aversion to self-kindness may be the fear of actually believing that you are good enough and engaging with the world as if you are. The very notion of liking—even loving—yourself exactly as you are is precisely the threat you're trying so desperately to avoid. As Marianne Williamson wrote in her book A *Return to Love*, "It is our light not our darkness that most frightens us."

What if you're terrified of your potential? What if that's why you silence your perspective, discount your experiences, and shrink yourself lest you take up too much space? If you've ever stayed quiet because the words you had to share didn't meet certain criteria (must be funny, witty, interesting, original), you've done exactly this. You've let the walls of self-criticism constrain you. Whereas others freely chat about the minutiae of their days, you scrutinize whether what you have to say is worth saying in the first place. You set limits on the extent to which you're allowed to try or achieve. While others pursue their musical passions despite never receiving any formal training, you stick to what you already know how to do—even if it enshrines a joyless existence. At every turn, you think twice, thrice, before you take a step. In doing so, you keep your wings tucked away while longingly admiring those who have found flight in the expansive sky.

This is the strange paradox of self-kindness—that you're scared of being kind to yourself because you might actually be worthy of it. So take some time to consider this: Are you afraid of being an abysmal failure, or are you afraid of being the fullest version of yourself you can be? Write down any thoughts or reactions you have to this question in your notebook.

The Benefits of Self-Kindness

We're getting ahead of ourselves, assuming that the goodness of self-kindness is self-evident when it's not, so we'll list what we see as the benefits of self-kindness. We're not trying to sell you on self-kindness; we're presenting what we know so you can make informed decisions. We hope that your choices will ultimately be about you and your values, not our reasons (seriously, don't take our word for it), because when push comes to shove, reasons crumble where values hold strong.

You save time and energy. The most obvious reason to practice self-kindness is energy conservation. Not only does feeding self-criticism take time and effort, but so does tussling with self-criticism to avoid sinking into a depressive rut. You lose both ways. Eventually, you find yourself in soul-sucking spirals of self-doubt, stoking the flames ("What if I really don't belong here and everyone is pretending to like me?") and then expending more energy trying to put out the fire ("Well then, why would they hire me in the first place?").

In contrast, self-kindness is about stepping away from the fire, sitting back in your camp chair, and watching the flames crackle and pop. Let go of the need to tend to the flame and instead direct your attention to the forest around you or anything on which you'd rather spend your energy. More concretely, self-kindness encourages you to notice the story your mind is used to telling ("...because I'm unlovable/broken/a failure")—even give a little nod to its history—and let it be. No piling on, no arguing, no reassuring. Let it be a story born of circumstance and nothing more.

You're more productive. A second reason to incorporate self-kindness into your life is that it increases productivity by decreasing avoidance. If you've often found your progress stymied by the fear of appearing incompetent or being wrong, self-kindness is the hall pass that says, "So what?" It pushes you to engage with the world in the face of uncertainty and declares that being wrong is perfectly okay.

The next time you find yourself in the refrigerated aisle of the grocery store, deliberating all the egg options—pasture-raised, free-range, cage-free, organic, grain-fed—practice self-kindness by giving yourself the grace of being a human being who will mess up at times. Instead of spending ten minutes weighing the pros and cons vis-à-vis industrial farming, the environment, animal welfare, and your budget, commit to a carton of eggs and trust that you're resilient enough to handle any potential guilt and self-blame (these are the actors we don't get to choose) that might arise from the choice. Self-kindness strips these thoughts and feelings of the power to keep you stuck in the grocery store for hours.

The same principle applies to finding routes on a map, selecting which dish to bring for a potluck, and devising a closet organization system. It's okay to act when you don't know the correct answer. You're much more likely to be productive when you let mistakes go and move on than if you ruminate on your shortcomings and get bogged down by indecisiveness.

You connect with others more authentically. The third reason to practice self-kindness is that it improves your ability to connect with others. It's difficult to be around someone who constantly denigrates themselves. Just as it's tiring for you to fend off self-criticism from every direction, it's wearying for others who feel pressured to provide reassurance—even if you don't ask for it—or who have heard the same self-blaming narrative numerous times before. When you accept yourself wholly, you not only get to connect with yourself as you are, but you also allow others to connect with you as you are. You give them the opportunity to truly see you, which is what so many of us yearn for at the end of the day. We all want to be seen. When you simply are, the people you care about can enjoy your presence and appreciate all of you.

At the same time, showing all of yourself is hard. Few of us eagerly open up ourselves to others. We've been conditioned to show our strongest side—when we're happy, healthy, and productive—and to hide or fix what we've come to define as weak: sadness, fear, low motivation, hopelessness. Recall the times you've been told, "Just smile," "Keep your chin up," "Don't worry," "Don't be stressed," or "Think positive." That's your conditioning. Consequently, when you feel stressed and overwhelmed, instead of reaching out, you retreat to your bubble so no one can see you be weak, so you aren't a burden, and so you can "fix" yourself. This is self-criticism saying you must meet certain criteria before you're permitted to interact with the world. By following this directive, you deprive yourself, just when you could use it the most, of one of your most basic needs: connection.

Self-kindness removes these stipulations. It says you get to participate in relationships even if you're suffering and you get to be around other people even if your mind labels you a "burden." Self-imposed isolation is harsh. (Isolation is literally a method of torture.) You wouldn't allow your children, friends, coworkers, or partner to talk to you only when they're feeling good about themselves, so why are you abiding by this rule?

There's also a curious irony about trying to connect by displaying your "strong" side. Think about it. In general, do you feel more connected to others when they're acing every challenge or when they're struggling with mundane tasks? Being better, smarter, quicker, prettier, stronger, and so forth creates a gulf between people by definition. The "-er" itself delineates separation between people through comparison. If one person is funnier, then both cannot be at the same place. Yet perfectionism keeps asking you to be more. What perfectionism is really asking for, then, is greater and greater distance between you and others.

Self-kindness asks for the opposite. It asks you to accept all parts of yourself, even—especially—the parts you don't like, and to give others the opportunity to do the same. Recall the last time you let someone see your supposed flaws: when you shared that you were scrambling to keep up with the other parents or feeling irritated over a petty matter. What was it like to present as you are, not as you believe you should be? The thing is, vulnerability doesn't make us weak; it makes us human. It gives us strength to be ourselves and to open our bubble to the world.

Assessment of Self-Kindness

Before we get to how to practice self-kindness, assess where you're at with self-kindness. Understanding your current behaviors and needs helps to determine what type of and how much self-kindness is going to be most beneficial for you. For example, if you have a hard time celebrating personal achievements, self-kindness could focus on recognizing and appreciating your talents. In contrast, if you avoid taking up space in group settings, then self-kindness may mean speaking up even when your mind tells you that you have nothing to contribute.

How do you treat yourself right now? What do you say to yourself when:

- You're having a hard time?

- You make careless mistakes?

- You state an opinion that later seems ignorant?

- You meet your goals?

- Others compliment you?

Run through the things you say to yourself in these situations and write them down in your notebook.

"Get over it." "Why are you so stupid?" "You're always messing up." "No one likes you." "Everyone thinks you're a burden." "You don't deserve to be here." "They're only saying nice things to be nice." Flip the perspective and picture saying those responses to someone other than yourself. Are they helpful responses?

Contemplate, too, what you allow and deny yourself. Do you give yourself permission to feel tired after chronically staying up late, to feel frustrated when things don't go your way, to have uncharitable thoughts about your closest friends, to forget an anniversary, to misunderstand your partner's intentions from time to time? Or do you guilt, shame, blame, and punish yourself when you believe you've fallen short? In your notebook, list two to three rules and expectations you have in this regard.

If you punish yourself, determine what that entails and evaluate how fair you're being. Do you skip dessert? Work out extra hard? Problem solve without any help? Reject assurances that everything is all right? Apologize profusely and then some more? Stay at home all weekend working? Maybe you lock yourself in the prison of your mind, feverishly reviewing all the reasons you're inadequate, recalling other painful memories that seemingly prove your worthlessness, and reminding yourself of all the people you've let down.

Even if your reaction is not entirely internally directed, consider that lashing out at those around you is also a form of self-punishment, because you're actively eroding the relationships you hold dear and dismantling the social network essential to your well-being. Imagine if someone told you to yell at your partner for folding laundry incorrectly or to make passive-aggressive comments to your coworker for messing up your filing system. Wouldn't that be cruel and unusual? Describe in your notebook two to three ways you punish yourself for breaking the rules or failing to meet expectations.

Practicing Self-Kindness

Now that you have a sense of how big (or little) of a role self-kindness plays in your life, let's get to how to practice it. Most self-kind actions are grounded in perspective taking, which, in turn, is rooted in the assumption that you are uniquely unkind to yourself. That is, you know how to be kind to others but fail to be kind to yourself.

With that in mind, we'll walk you through a perspective-taking exercise (also available in audio format as "Practicing Self-Kindness" at http://www.newharbinger.com/48459). Try to make the exercise as immersive as possible by adding detail, checking in with all five senses, and keeping your spotlight focused on the exercise. You might even think to yourself, "I don't have time for this exercise. I only gave myself fifteen minutes to read this chapter tonight." What do you think we're going to ask you to do with that thought? Refrain from arguing with or listening to it. Take it as a prompt to show yourself some kindness.

Start by thinking of someone you care for unconditionally. This is someone who literally can't do anything to make you love them less, not even if they miss your birthday, cancel plans at the last minute, or repeatedly mispronounce your child's name—you would still love them just as much (though you may certainly feel annoyed with them in the moment).

What shows up for you when you visualize this person? Close your eyes. Notice what changes occur in your body.

...

...

...

Did your heart beat faster? Was there fluttering or lightness in your chest? Did you sense goose bumps? We typically have a certain physiological reaction to the people we love. Experience what it is like to choose love in this moment. Take time to settle into the glow of it. Observe your love reaching the person you've visualized and let them bask in its warmth.

...

...

...

Now replace that person with you. Picture yourself on the receiving end of this loving energy. Do your best to maintain focus and reorient to the exercise if you get distracted. What is it like to look at yourself through this lens? Can you allow yourself to receive the love you give? Write your observations and reactions in your notebook.

Looking at yourself in this way can provide powerful guidance for how to practice self-kindness. If you saw yourself suffering through loving eyes, what would you do? Think of how you would treat the person you love. If they believed they were unlovable, would you agree with them and demand they prove that they deserve your love? If they were overwhelmed with stress and anxiety, would you tell them to get over it and try harder? If they were worried about what others thought of them, would you advise them to act like a different person to be more likable? We're guessing no.

You'd be more likely to give them a hug and reiterate that the self-stories, worries, and self-doubt don't affect how much you love them. If the person asked you why you love them in spite of all their shortcomings, you might find the question ludicrous. Intuitively, you know that you love them simply because you choose to and because you do. You don't need to justify your love, just as you don't need to justify your values. In fact, loving *is* a value. You have the power to do it, it's bigger than a goal, and it colors your life in unimaginable ways. In other words, your loving this person is a meaningful *choice*; loving and being kind are within your control.

The point we're trying to make is that you *already* know how to practice self-kindness because you know how to be kind to others. The crux is doing the same for yourself and appreciating the breadth of self-kindness. Here are a few ways to practice self-kindness:

- Ask for help

- Be vulnerable with people you trust

- Create space for difficult thoughts and feelings

- Find a new hobby or get back into an old one

- Get enough sleep

- Go to therapy

- Opt out of activities that don't serve you or your values

- Prioritize your needs over those of others

- Set and maintain personal boundaries (for example, say no to extraneous favors)

- State your needs explicitly

- Surround yourself with people who love and respect you

- Take time to eat and savor meals

At the same time, knowing what to do to take care of yourself doesn't ameliorate emotional barriers. That's where taking a loving perspective toward yourself comes in. What's it like to take the stance that you are someone worth caring about?

If you struggle to look at yourself with kindness and gentleness, *pretend* you do. You can only start from where you are, and if that's where you are, start there. Act as if you care about yourself, your well-being, and your contentment. Remember, loving and being kind to yourself are values, which means you can *choose* self-kindness—whether you believe you deserve it, whether it makes you feel good, or whether you can justify it. We expect the pretending to turn into genuine caring, because we believe you'll naturally gravitate toward the version of your life awash with self-kindness over the one without it. Test this out for yourself by pretending to care. Give self-kindness a fair shot and see if you like the results.

We acknowledge our bias here. If we could choose for you, we'd want you to make self-kindness a value, but we can't. We're partial because we've seen people blossom through self-nurturance and interacting with parts of the world from which they had previously barred themselves. We've seen people fail to find the words to adequately capture how different their lives are once they embrace self-kindness. The transformative power of self-kindness is remarkable. As you share love with yourself, you accept love from and build connections with others. When you recognize that relentless self-criticism, shame, and guilt are products of your history—not reflections of reality—you free yourself from the clutches of perfectionism. In doing so, you become empowered to seize each day and live for yourself. So, from our biased perch, self-kindness is more than a choice—it's an imperative.

✻ ✻ ✻

We advocate for self-kindness out of necessity, not indulgence. As much as your mind shames or guilts you into forsaking your emotional and physical well-being for some other more "productive" pursuit, we encourage you to take the time, energy, and space to care for yourself.

Self-kindness doesn't have to be elaborate; it can be eating breakfast, listening to your favorite song, or going to bed by 10:00 p.m. In fact, self-kindness is more helpful when practiced consistently than sporadically. The benefits of self-kindness include saving precious energy otherwise spent worrying and ruminating, increasing productivity (likely in a different way from how perfectionism means it), and more genuinely connecting with the people around you.

To practice self-kindness, view and treat yourself how you would a loved one. Notice if the urge to justify self-kindness shows up and wave it along; the question of whether you're adequately deserving is moot. You can value being kind to yourself just because, like you can value being outside or going on adventures.

With all the tools laid out in this part of the book, in the next two chapters we now turn to strategies for translating skills into actual behavioral changes.

CHAPTER 9

Living the Life You Want

A Jedi Grand Master once said, "Do or do not. There is no try." There's an elegance in this simplistic dichotomy: when rubber meets the road, we either act or stagnate. As an example, *trying* to do your laundry is sitting on your bed and looking over at the pile of dirty clothes occupying its designated corner of the room. *Doing* your laundry is putting your clothes in the washer, taking them out of the dryer, and folding them.

Whether you acknowledge it or not, you're *always* doing or not doing (this includes trying) with respect to a specific goal. You can continue to *try* to accept that you will make mistakes, or you can do it. You can *try* to orient yourself toward your values instead of unfair expectations and externally imposed standards, or you can do it. Note how these paths diverge.

So this chapter is about walking the walk and applying the skills we've discussed so far. The aims are to identify specific behavioral goals tied to your values and outline strategies to help you kick-start new behavioral patterns.

SMART Goals

If you've done any behavioral therapy or management training, you've probably heard of SMART goals. Or, as someone who thought this book was relevant to them, you may already be setting SMART goals. SMART goals are key to behavior change; they're a method of devising goals that increases your chances of meeting them. That is, the SMART formula gives you a leg up even before you act on your actual goals. SMART stands for:

- Specific

- Measurable

- Achievable

- Relevant

- Time-bound

Here's how to use SMART goals to undermine perfectionism.

Specific. Specific means the goal is concrete and sufficiently detailed, such that an observer would be able to tell that you were working on the goal. If you can easily visualize what the action looks like based on the description of the goal, you're on track. For example, "go for a run outside" is specific (we know exactly what running outside looks like), whereas "exercise" is not (this could be yoga, ultimate Frisbee, Pilates, or tennis). "Go for a run outside" can be even more specific: "go for a run in Sugar House Park." Similarly, "improve leadership style" is vague. A more specific goal would be: "provide performance feedback to coworkers and give suggestions for behavior change in weekly one-on-one meetings." To make a goal even more concrete, add the day of the week on which it will be met.

A common trap we all fall into with goals is framing them as a "don't" or "do less of": Don't procrastinate (or procrastinate less). Don't be late. Don't take on more projects. These are dead-person goals in that a cadaver can accomplish them simply by lying there. An issue with "don't" goals is that what you want change is unclear. Think of when people tell you to not snap at them. Sure, you can do that, but what do they want you to do instead? Do you leave the room, describe how you're feeling in the moment, or repeat your request more politely? Framing the goal as an active action makes it easier to grasp what your next steps are.

Thus, when you think about the *specific* criterion, make sure you can visualize what you need to do—not what you need to not do.

Measurable. Measurable means the behavior can be quantified and has a discrete end point; that is, you know when the goal is completed. Measurement is usually done in terms of frequency, duration, or a binary yes/no. How you choose to measure the behavior depends on what makes the most sense given where you're at and what you're working to change. For instance, if I were an ultramarathon runner, my goal might be to "go for a *twenty-mile* run," whereas if the last time I put on running shoes was fifteen years ago, I might aim to "run *around the block once*" (the italics show the measurable part of the goal). Alternatively, if I don't really care about distance and am more concerned with being outside for a requisite amount of time for vitamin D exposure, I would make my goal to "go for a *fifteen-minute* run." There's no rule about what type of measurement is best; it all depends on the context of your goals.

An advantage of quantifying goals is that you sidestep any back-and-forth you might otherwise have with your mind about what the goal entails. A specific and measurable goal is unambiguous; it's a fifteen-minute walk regardless of whether or not you feel tired, it's raining, or you exercised the day before. In addition, quantifying goals gives you an objective metric by which to judge completion. Especially with perfectionism, you're liable to say you didn't quite meet the goal and withhold recognition until you reach the impossible, ever-shifting bar.

Achievable. Achievable refers to setting realistic goals. This can be difficult for perfectionists, who are used to setting high expectations for themselves—even more so when they frequently meet the high expectations. In these cases, what is "realistic" becomes more and more untenable: if you got promoted twice within the first three years of your job, then you might believe it's "realistic" for you to be promoted at least once more in the next few years. However, this extrapolation fails to account for the sleep you lost to late work nights and relationships withering from neglect. So is the goal actually reasonable? Setting goals in this way is like expecting Tim Duncan to make a buzzer-beating three-pointer every single game. Just because you've done something once—or even a few times—doesn't make it realistic.

Especially when you're first drafting SMART goals, we recommend starting off with offensively easy goals—to the point where you feel patronized. Think of this principle similarly to gaining momentum with a heavy boulder. You would start moving the boulder by inching it in the desired direction (this is the hardest part), but once it gets going, you can rely on inertia to help keep it in motion. By "easy," we mean the probability of success should be at least 95 percent. Hence, if you're feeling overwhelmed by the zillion and one tasks on your to-do list, your goal won't be to check everything off. You're not even going to pick a moderately difficult task. You're going to start with the easiest possible step. If that's rewriting or even coming up with your to-do list, do that. If it's replying to a text, do that. If it's taking a shower, then that's your goal. No step is too small; a step toward your values is a step closer to your values.

Breaking down projects or tasks like this can be challenging for the perfectionist who is wedded to an all-or-nothing mindset: If you can't get all of it done, why bother? If you can't get through your entire morning routine of brushing your teeth, washing your face, getting dressed, making breakfast, eating breakfast, and packing lunch, you might as well sleep in and roll into work late. You might also have an all-or-nothing rule about having to see a project to completion once you start it, so you keep attempting to set aside chunks of time for uninterrupted progress. However, the weekend to clear out your basement or afternoon to organize your tax documents doesn't materialize, and you're still stuck on zero progress.

When you feel pulled toward all-or-nothing thinking, breathe and notice those rules floating about your mind space. Perfectionism decrees, "There's no point in doing things halfway." Look at the rule for what it is: a thought, a suggestion, an opinion. See if you observe anything else getting in the way of starting. You might notice discomfort around leaving the task incomplete or not doing it exactly how you would've liked. Reflect on whether listening to these rules and feelings serves your values. What would happen if you chose to leave them be?

The fact is, 50 percent completion is more than 0 percent completion. Yes, 100 percent is more than 50 percent, but if we're focusing on *achievable* goals, then striving for 100 percent all the time is unsustainable. You know this. Moreover, 50 percent completed means 50 percent left to do as opposed to 100 percent. Of course, writing a beautiful report with perfectly aligned tables and neat figures would be preferable to turning in a mediocre one. At the same time, turning in a mediocre product is preferable to letting another deadline slip by or skipping weekend plans with your family to finesse the report.

The perfect performance is a mirage; that's why we can grasp and grasp and still never reach it. Instead, take the 50 percent, or 75 percent, or 30 percent and call it a win. Each of those scenarios still beats 0 percent. We're asking you to start small, but that's not where you'll end. Just like with learning to walk, you'll find each subsequent step easier and easier to take. You'll fall several times as you navigate new terrain. It's all part of the growing process, so embrace falling. Eventually, you'll be leaping and bounding toward your values. It's just that building those muscles and endurance takes time.

Relevant. Relevant means the goal matters to *you*. This criterion eliminates goals based on shoulds, which are often about external expectations. Whereas people's expectations of us are neither good nor bad from a psychological standpoint, the problem is that people want us to do many things. They want us—or we think they want us—to respond to emails immediately, agree with them, speak up in meetings, speak less in meetings, compliment their haircuts, and be fun at parties.

When our natural inclination is to act according to shoulds, assessing relevance requires clarity and honesty. That's clarity of perspective: Are you clearly seeing the link between this goal and your values? Are you clearly seeing your values through the fog of thoughts and feelings? Then be honest with yourself. Choose goals that matter to you, even if the people around you disapprove of them. Abstain from endeavors people prescribe for you if you know that they don't actually matter to you. Stipulating relevant goals is tough, and you might choose to follow a should now and again (that's being flexible). However, at the end of the day, realize that each action you take is a star in the constellation of your life and be intentional about the shape of the constellation you're creating.

Now, the perfectionistic part of your mind might be struggling to commit to new behaviors, questioning if they're really "worth it." Or it might be launching into "optimize mode" and urging you to pick the "most efficient and productive" goals, which may not actually be *relevant* ones. This is what your mind does: it wants to problem solve, even when there isn't a problem that needs solving. Rather than get entangled with the need to optimize, choose goals that have some meaning to you or find meaning in the activity you choose. If you commit to selecting a hotel in less than an hour, connect with the idea that doing this will give you many free hours during which you can read a book, get tea with a friend, or play with your child—as opposed to spending hours asking for advice from family and friends, scouring different travel websites, and creating a monster spreadsheet.

Time-bound. Time-bound refers to setting a deadline for your goal and sticking to it. Deadlines are anathema to procrastination, which is why adhering to them once you've set them is crucial. Without a deadline, you can drag out specific, measurable, achievable, relevant goals for years, buying into disingenuous thoughts like "I'll get to them," "I'm working on them," or "Now is not the best time." You might have done this with household chores, leaving light bulbs waiting to be replaced, boxes of old clothes collecting dust in the garage, and plants begging to be repotted. It's much easier to put off tasks when you aren't accountable to others, so you do.

Assigning a deadline also makes it clear when you've failed, which makes deadlines scary. An undefined time limit allows us to procrastinate not only the task but also failure. As long as you're "still working on it," you haven't technically failed. As long as there's a *chance* of completion, you can still succeed. Deadlines close this loophole; they stamp INCOMPLETE on your assignment if you don't finish it by the specified hour. If you don't book your flight to go home for the holidays two weeks before your departure date, you've failed. Respecting a deadline requires commitment, part of which means committing to the possibility of failure.

Deadlines are helpful for the same reason they are daunting. Because they signal a time limit, they keep you from laboring over a project that could go on forever if you let it. For example, tests with unlimited duration seem like a fine idea. You can be assured that you'll have ample time to shade bubbles cleanly, plan out your written responses, edit your essays, and double-check your calculations. But imagine what unlimited duration would do to a perfectionistic mind that always finds something that can be done better: "Okay, I'm done with the test and checked all my answers, but why don't I check them again since I have time? Maybe write an alternative response and compare them to see which one more adequately satisfies the prompt. Did I check for spelling errors? Did I read each question carefully in case I got confused by the double-negative questions?" This can go on indefinitely, and you can do this with pretty much anything. Without a deadline on a manuscript, researchers can spend months writing and refining drafts while the science moves past what they have to contribute. Without a deadline on a home-improvement project, you can leave paint cans in the living room unopened, waiting until the mood to paint strikes.

However, eventually, you need to either get things done or let them go. Living in a limbo of procrastination and technical nonfailures is like standing on the threshold between two rooms. You feel stuck on an old task and can't completely immerse yourself in new tasks since you continue to be on the hook for something that constantly lingers in the back of your mind. Maybe you've been meaning to start knitting a sweater. Then you glimpse the wilted piles of knotted wool still waiting to be turned into scarves and decide against it. You remain on the threshold.

It would be nicer to step into the new room and start afresh, yet closing the door behind you is difficult. It means acknowledging that you won't finish something you started (or meant to start). For that, your mind labels you a "failure" or a "quitter." Now, is it more helpful to respond to the label as if it were important, or to notice the label, take a step back, and connect with your values? Make space for the discomfort of incompletion if it means you get to take a step toward something you truly care about.

In actuality, quitting is not a sign of weakness; it can be a sign of wisdom and self-kindness. Just as you'd ask a loved one driving in a snowstorm to pull over or turn back instead of pressuring them to finish their journey, you can allow yourself to stop engaging in work that doesn't serve your needs and values.

Conversely, if there's meaningful work to be done in the previous room, return to it. Do what's good for you. Perhaps you'll instead need to be open to the distress of not getting things done perfectly or the sense of being overwhelmed by all the work that needs to be done. Notice the hubbub: all the rooms you could be in, all the rooms you have been in. Breathe all the way through your body. Can you experience all that and still *choose* to move toward what matters?

Remember the A in SMART: achievable. We're not asking you to sprint toward the finish line if you're still warming up. We're asking you to find the smallest possible step in the chaos. Define it. Measure it. Set a time limit. Take it.

Setting Your Goals

The SMART criteria form the foundation of goal setting. All letters in the acronym are important, but we suggest starting with your (relevant) values when setting goals. Sometimes, you may be so concerned about your next step that you forget your destination. If you don't know where you want to go, how do you define progress? So work backward. Start from where you want to end up (values), draw a metaphorical line to where you're currently at, and then decide on what next actions make sense for you.

For example, if your value is to better the world, reflect on areas where this is most meaningful to you. Let's say work, family, and friends stand out. Explore how you could better the world in each of those areas. For work, you may choose to be more accepting of mistakes and turn assignments in on time versus procrastinating or only submitting flaw-less work. For family, you may choose to be more spontaneous when your partner or children want to change plans at the last minute. For friends, you may focus on being more present and actively listening when you're with them rather than worrying about your to-do list. This method of funneling broad values to specific SMART goals keeps you tethered to your values, which is especially helpful if you're apt to get distracted by the trees in the forest.

Even after you formulate initial goals, understand that goals are changeable and probably will change as you learn new information, find new interests, clarify your values, and grow. Identifying personal goals is about having a snapshot of the path you want to forge. At any point in time, it's helpful to know roughly where you're headed. However, the snapshot can't account for capricious conditions and human variability, and rigidly clinging to an outdated snapshot that was correct at the time it was developed can be detrimental. If you're hiking in the woods, it's useful to know immediate next steps and general future steps as you make your way along the trail. If nothing deviates from what you expect, you can even adhere to your plan until you reach the peak of the mountain. However, fallen trees, wasp nests, ambiguous growling noises, gray clouds, and a rumbling stomach can all throw a wrench into your plans. If you still want to get to the top, you need to adapt. Notice that your overall direction remains the same (that is, still toward your values), but your path there may change.

With that said, in your notebook, list two or three current goals linked to your values (these could be those you identified in chapter 6 or different ones). You're welcome to add more later, but let's start small. Check them against the SMART criteria. Are they specific, measurable, achievable, relevant, and time-bound? Edit them if they aren't. Make sure each goal is clearly defined.

Now that you have a set of SMART goals in front of you, categorize them as small, medium, or large. Typically, "size" is determined by corresponding effort or timeline. Effort and timeline may be correlated but are not always: you may have high-effort goals with a short timeline, like a last-minute job application, or a low-effort goal with an extended timeline, like going through your children's old clothes over months. Determine which category best matches each goal.

Taking a big-picture perspective on your goals by sorting them provides guidance on how to efficiently pursue them, where you have space to add more, and which ones to drop. For instance, you may realize that you have only large, long-term goals, which may explain why you constantly feel like you're pursuing something far away. In this case, add smaller, shorter-term goals along the way so that you know if you're on track and can more frequently contact a sense of accomplishment. Although cultural messaging tells you that working for a delayed reward is a sign of self-discipline, doing so tends to destabilize progress and makes your journey more onerous than it needs to be. In essence, you're making things harder for yourself by delaying gratification.

Once you have a better sense of the distribution of your goals, identify gaps in your list. Are you missing longer-term goals that give you a sense of striving and meaning? Are you missing smaller goals that will help you generate momentum for bigger goals? You can add new goals now or later. For now, it's more important to have a working list of goals so that the rest of the chapter will still feel applicable.

Pitter-Patter, Let's Get at 'Er

Knowing how to define goals and identifying your goals are the first steps. The next step is using behavioral strategies to increase your likelihood of following through on goals. Think of your behavior as the product of an ever-changing scale of probability. Certain variables increase probability (like wearing workout clothes to sleep for exercising the next morning), and others decrease probability (like going to bed at 2:00 a.m. for a 7:00 a.m. gym class). However, the thing about probability is that you can't guarantee behaviors. For example, gathering your tax documents, firing up your tax preparation software, and clicking "Begin" doesn't guarantee you'll file your taxes—you're just much more likely to do it in this context than others. Nonetheless, it's empowering to exercise control over probabilities and increase the likelihood of valued behaviors while decreasing the likelihood of unhealthy behaviors, rather than feel subject to the whims of your feelings and circumstances. Each strategy listed below helps you do just that.

Structure your environment. *Stimulus control* describes the phenomenon in which behavior is controlled by the presence or absence of a given stimulus. For example, you're more likely to watch *The Americans* in the presence of a television set and less likely to eat chocolate if you don't have any around the house. With respect to behavior change, you can leverage stimulus control to structure your environment to maximize the occurrence of helpful behaviors and minimize that of unhelpful behaviors. In other words, you can arrange your environment to set yourself up for success.

Note that "environment" refers to all parts of your context, including your inner landscape (such as feeling tired). There is no set formula for successful stimulus control, because the stimulus to manipulate depends on the behavior you want to change, which depends on your goals, which, in turn, depend on your values. Here, we'll describe how stimulus control works, and then let you figure out what moves make sense given your understanding of which factors influence your behaviors. The components of stimulus control are:

1. Identify the behavior of interest or the behavior you want to change.

2. Consider which variables are most likely to influence the behavior.

3. Use problem-solving skills to determine what alterations to the environment will most effectively support desired behavior change.

4. Implement the manipulations and see what happens.

5. Make adjustments based on the results of your testing. Return to step 2 if you need to reanalyze the situation and identify other influential variables or to step 3 if the issue is figuring out a different way to manipulate the variables you've already identified.

As an example, let's say you're procrastinating replying to an email from your supervisor. Instead, you watch videos of surprised puppies and Broadway musical parodies. Let's walk through the steps.

1. There are two behaviors of interest: (1) emailing your supervisor and (2) watching internet videos. Presumably, you want to do the first behavior and stop the second.

2. Identify variables that make you (1) more likely to write the email (having your in-box open versus having multiple windows and tabs open) and (2) less likely to watch videos (closing your internet browser windows open to video websites).

3. Weighing these options, you could close all other desktop applications besides your email or install an app to prevent you from opening distracting websites (these apps are based on the premise of stimulus control, by erecting barriers to unwanted behaviors). You want to shift the odds in your favor by making it easier for you to send the email (by already having a blank email open) and more difficult to watch the videos (by making them inaccessible). When I, Mike, want to focus on writing, I'll work with my office door open so people walking by can see if I'm browsing the internet, which makes me less likely to escape to Reddit.

4. Observe if you end up sending the email.

5. If so, congratulations. You successfully used stimulus control. If not, return to step 2 to redefine the problem or step 3 to brainstorm alternative solutions.

As you devise ways to modify your surroundings, it's useful to know that, because of our language abilities, stimuli can have *arbitrary* effects on us. This is another reason why there's no recipe for stimulus control; the same stimulus has different functions depending on the person, their history, and their context. For instance, in response to a scarf, some of us may recall a lost grandparent and feel sad, others may feel excited to use it as winter approaches, and others may feel stressed as it reminds them of their unfinished crochet project. Anything can take on any meaning as long as you make the relevant mental associations (scarf → grandparent → death → loss → sadness).

Understanding these arbitrary relations and how they shape the function of stimuli is helpful, because if you appreciate how the associations work and influence your behaviors, you can use their powers to your advantage. For example, if you know that the image of an überfit climber like Adam Ondra is going to motivate you to exercise regularly, add that to your environment. If you know that setting the background of your phone screen to your family's dog will remind you to call your parents more often, do that. Capitalize on the arbitrariness.

Another corollary of our language abilities is that we're able to respond to *cognitive* or *verbal* stimuli, like rules, self-stories, anxiety, and depression, when most animals respond only to physical stimuli. Try it out. Picture the most decadent chocolate cake with thick, creamy frosting and airy sponge layers. Really picture it. Notice how you're reacting to this image. Maybe you're salivating and want to get some cake right now such that you're more likely to buy a cake or eat the one already in your fridge. Your dog and polar bears can't do this.

Our ability to respond to verbal stimuli means we can use them as part of stimulus control. One of the more significant applications of this is shifting behavioral probabilities by *becoming aware* of values and current patterns of prioritization. That is, you may act differently depending on whether you're *aware of* your values and the priorities your actions reflect. Choosing to check your email over watching your children play at the park is easier to do when you don't realize you're implicitly prioritizing emotional avoidance (in this case, avoiding the anxiety of unread emails) over being a present parent. However, being aware of the discrepancy between your values and your actions may make you more likely to choose parenting over avoidance.

Awareness is about making *informed* decisions; you're adding information to your environment to sway probabilities. Will you be more likely to try to alleviate anxiety when you realize it takes you further away from your values or more likely to play with your children to be the parent you want to be?

Introduce consequences. Another behavioral method is *contingency management*, which broadly refers to using operant conditioning (that is, reinforcement and punishment) to alter behavior. In the context of intervention, it usually refers specifically to the use of *rewards* to shape behavior (positive reinforcement). This approach is intuitive to most people. Reward a behavior and see more of it; punish a behavior and see less of it. The less intuitive parts are that (1) reinforcement can entail the *removal* of something aversive (negative reinforcement), and (2) punishment is unfavorable for behavior change in the long run—another reason why self-criticism is harmful over time. The implications of these principles are that you have more options in terms of how to reinforce behaviors (like setting an obnoxious alarm so you're more likely to get up to turn it off) and that you can leave out punishment.

Contingency management still works in the realm of probabilities. Introducing particular consequences makes certain behaviors more or less likely. If you give yourself a cookie for vacuuming, you're more likely to do it. If you notice that your stress tends to decrease after vacuuming (removal of aversive stimulus), you're also more likely to do it. However, you can't make your stress go away as easily as you can make the cookie happen, so trying to implement negative reinforcement with stress as the aversive consequence is impractical. Contingency management strategies need to center on consequences we can directly manipulate, like dessert.

In addition, it's generally more sustainable to support behavior change with rewards than with threats of unpleasant outcomes. Compare running to get ice cream to running away from a grizzly bear. For this reason, we lean toward focusing on positive reinforcement, though negative reinforcement can certainly be helpful at times (for example, putting your trash bags next to the front door so you're more likely to take them outside).

The key points of contingency management are to:

1. Tie rewards to objectively defined goals

2. Select rewards that are genuinely reinforcing

3. Clearly define the rewards

For the first point, SMART goals will get you most of the way there. The remaining portion relies on you noting when you have completed the goal and administering the reward, which can be tricky. For instance, have you ever thought about all the gaming you'll reward yourself with once you finish a huge project…only to be so exhausted at the end of it or immediately hooked by the next item on your to-do list that you end up forgetting to celebrate? For contingency management to work, you need to follow through on the promised consequence. If forgetting is the issue, add reminders and prompts (that's stimulus control). If you can't tell when you've met your goal, return to the SMART criteria. Most likely, your goal wasn't measurable.

The second piece is that rewards need to be properly gratifying. If you don't actually care about reading Michelle Obama's biography, then "rewarding" yourself by purchasing *Becoming* won't change the likelihood of any behavior. You're too smart to lie to yourself, so pick rewards you genuinely find rewarding. Rewards can be tangible, like a burrito, a new snowboard, or a limited-edition Boba Fett action figure. They can also be intangible, like quality time with loved ones, sanctioned procrastination time, watching *Fleabag*, or permission to skip a boring gathering—get creative. Rewards adhere to the principle of function over form, so they need to serve the function of being positively reinforcing (that is, they increase the likelihood of the desired behavior) rather than simply appearing enticing.

Finally, rewards need to be specific, just like goals. Are you getting one or three donuts? Where will you get the donuts? What flavor donuts will you get? Being specific from the start saves you from arguing with yourself later on about how much of the reward you really deserve, even if attaining the goal was easier than you expected.

Pretend you're signing a contract with yourself: agree to the terms and execute it as stipulated. For example, I, Mike, reward myself with finishing my tasks for the day by going for a bike ride once I'm done. Even if I wrap things up at 2:00 p.m. and my mind tells me I have time to write more paragraphs, I don't add work or meetings. I head out early and enjoy the fresh mountain air.

Be accountable. The third strategy to improve your chances of successful behavior change is accountability. Hold yourself—or have someone hold you—to your commitments. It sounds straightforward, and it mostly is. You state your goal and make sure you follow through. The primary purpose of accountability is to increase motivation, just like fasting increases your motivation to eat. Here, "motivation" describes a state in which the target behavior is more likely to occur; we don't mean it as a feeling. We define motivation as a state under the influence of certain environmental factors, because that increases your control over your level of motivation. Thus, you can put on disco tunes to increase your motivation to work out or tell someone you'll meet them for lunch to increase your motivation to get out of the house. In therapy, clients often tell us that knowing we'll ask about how their homework went helps them to do it, suggesting they're physically and cognitively able to complete the tasks; they just need extra incentive in the form of accountability. This is the *intended* effect of accountability.

However, accountability may have the opposite effect of decreasing motivation or creating a state in which you're less likely to do the target behavior. For example, it may add stress and make goals feel more overwhelming, leading to avoidance. The variable effect of accountability has to do with how we arbitrarily assign meaning to stimuli, such that the same stimulus can have a range of effects (recall the discussion of arbitrary relations earlier in this chapter). Emphasizing function over form means attending to these arbitrary effects. So if accountability promotes avoidance, find a way to make it motivating or skip this strategy altogether; there are other ways to shift probabilities. Conversely, if you lack the skills to complete a task, accountability is not the answer. Rather, use skills acquisition, help seeking, and problem solving to meet your goal.

For public commitments with other people holding you accountable, pick people you respect, are close to, or care about, so the accountability will hold more weight. You're more likely to follow through if you made an agreement with your child's godparent than with the hairdresser you see once a year. For example, I, Clarissa, used to email my graduate school adviser, Mike, project updates every Monday. Doing so helped me to keep track of the status of different projects and served as a weekly check-in for myself in case I let things slide off my plate. The emails kept me engaged in my work and more likely to move projects along, but you may be the kind of person for whom emailing weekly updates to an authority figure only fuels procrastination. If so, do it differently. Pick someone who feels encouraging or space out your updates. Do whatever will make you *more likely* to follow through on tasks.

For personal accountability, rigidity may come in handy. Be rigid about respecting deadlines and honoring commitments. If you said noon on Wednesday, it's noon on Wednesday—not late afternoon or midnight, not Thursday because you had a headache on Wednesday. Rigidity can be helpful (ironically) because shifting deadlines and altering stated commitments can be forms of avoidance. For example, you may push back a personal deadline to *avoid* guilt related to missing yet another deadline. Cutting yourself slack here and there may be insignificant when considered in isolation, but it contributes to a broader pattern of structuring your environment to accommodate avoidance. As you become proficient at meeting deadlines and being accountable to yourself, introduce flexibility, understanding that flexibility is about being adaptive when life happens, not an excuse for procrastination.

Rigid accountability has a different function from rigid adherence to expectations. The former is about sticking to plans you've decided are good for you based on your values, whereas the latter is about sticking to arbitrary standards disconnected from your values. It's the difference between setting multiple alarms to ensure you wake up on time to prepare for your sibling's wedding and setting multiple alarms to ensure you attend a 5:00 a.m. gym class because it's on your schedule. The *purpose* of rigidity matters. When it comes to holding yourself accountable, use the force of rigidity for good.

Barriers to Change

Besides using behavioral strategies to keep yourself on track toward your goals and values, it's also helpful to be aware of obstacles that will likely show up so you can anticipate and deftly navigate them.

The busyness trap. A common roadblock is the "I'm too busy" rhetoric. You have too many things on your plate right now. You'd love to try out these skills but don't have time in your packed schedule. Once work eases up, though, you'll definitely dedicate time to practice mindfulness. We get it. Our minds tell us the same thing. It's too easy to get sucked into the vortex of busyness and live in the narrative that you "don't have time" for anything other than what you're already doing. It might even feel frustrating to want to try out new things and be unable to eke out time in your day.

However, what's really happening is that your mind is promoting a false perception that busyness is *imposed*—that you are made to be busy by forces outside your control and that you, therefore, can't escape the busyness. Your mind tells you, as a matter of fact, that you don't have time to get coffee with your spouse or make elaborate home-cooked meals. It reiterates that if you spend time on "unproductive" activities like these, you're taking away precious time from something more constructive, like planning out your week or decluttering your desktop. Your perfectionistic mind might even have prepared rules for you to follow: you can't miss deadlines (that's Mike), you need to catalog all your tasks in your task management app (that's Clarissa), or you have to stay on top of every single project (still Clarissa). Thus, even when you value *both* relationships and work, following perfectionistic rules can lead you to disproportionately be busy with work at the expense of your marriage.

Instead of buying into the "I'm too busy" narrative, think of busyness as a way for you to signal your priorities in the moment, which means you *do* have control over your busyness. Busyness is about what you choose to make room for in your life just as much as it's about what you're sacrificing to create that space, even if both are consistent with your values—that's why busyness is about prioritizing. For example, you'd never be "too busy" to visit a dying relative at the hospital or take your dog to the vet for a medical emergency.

When you say you're "too busy" to do something, what you're really saying is "I'm not willing to make time for this right now." If you're "too busy" to call your parents, you're saying that you're not willing to make time to connect with them right now. If you're "too busy" to go to therapy, you're saying you're not willing to make time to take care of your mental health right now. You don't consciously think of these implications, but they're what your actions demonstrate. In a sense, "too busy" is a state your mind made up to keep you constrained within certain boundaries. Thankfully, you have the power to *make time* for things that matter to you, even if your mind says you can't afford to do so.

In your notebook, write down two to three activities you're "too busy" to do, like eat lunch or call up an old friend. Use the format: "I'm too busy to _____ right now."

Next, replace "too busy" with "not willing to make time," so your statement now reads: "I'm not willing to make time to _____ right now." Here are a few examples:

- "I'm not willing to make time to *sleep eight hours a night* right now."

- "I'm not willing to make time to *get regular exercise* right now."

- "I'm not willing to make time to *take my medication as prescribed* right now."

Now read your statements back to yourself, fully appreciating their meaning. Do you agree with your revised statements? If you do, you're prioritizing exactly as you want to, so you're good there. If you disagree, that means your actions are inconsistent with your priorities. Everyone does this.

As discussed earlier regarding stimulus control, your *awareness* of this incongruity makes you more likely to change. You can make your choices reflect your values more equitably. Be flexible when rules about what you "don't have time for" pop up, and be intentional about which values you choose to follow in the moment. Know that, regardless of how "busy" your mind says you are, you absolutely can choose what you do with your time.

The need for certainty. Another barrier to change is perfectionism's demand for certainty before action. Because perfectionism says you need to know that your goal is correct before you spend any time or energy on it, you can get stuck spending weeks and months trying to figure out if your goal is worth pursuing in the first place. The issue with making certainty a prerequisite for action is that you *can't* be sure you're making the right choice. There are too many unknown variables, especially if these are new actions you're adding to your repertoire. In effect, perfectionism is asking you to seek a certainty that doesn't exist.

Rather than get caught up in what's right, make a choice and follow through on it—even if your mind is yelling at you to reconsider. This will require intention and all the skills you've learned in previous chapters; it's more than "just do it." *After* you've engaged in the chosen action, reflect on how it worked for you. Do you want more days like that? Do you wish you had done things differently? What would you have done differently?

Use the feedback from your experience to guide future choices. Assessing the action after it's completed gives you the advantage of hindsight and space from the mental noise to more fairly assess your decision. Trying to evaluate an action while doing it, with your mind already doubting—even belittling—your decision can get unwieldy.

Even after the action, your perfectionistic mind may still nudge you toward endless second-guessing about whether you *really* made the right choice. If this happens, acknowledge the chatter and give yourself more time to create distance from the event. This could be hours or days. Do what you need to do to move yourself along—this means living in the present and according to your values. You can return to assessing when you gain some clarity.

The function of following through on goals is not to be right; it's to practice doing behaviors that are consistent with your values. Imagine what your life would look like if you got really skilled at meeting your goals regardless of what perfectionism threw at you. How much bigger would your world be?

* * *

Walking the walk is more complicated than putting one foot in front of the other. There are ways to make it easier, like using the SMART (specific, measurable, achievable, relevant, time-bound) criteria when setting goals. After you've defined your goals, increase your likelihood of following through on them by (1) structuring your environment to encourage desirable behaviors and discourage undesirable behaviors; (2) rewarding yourself for values-consistent behaviors; and (3) holding yourself or having someone hold you accountable for meeting your goals. By using these strategies, you're giving yourself the best chance at changing your behavior and relying less on waiting for your mood to shift.

As you work on your goals, perfectionism will cast doubt every step of the way; that's expected. Complete what you set out to do and use what you learn from your experiences to decide what you want to do in the future. In the next chapter, we discuss how to retain and build on positive changes you make—especially in a world that will never stop asking you to be perfect.

CHAPTER 10

Staying on the Path You've Chosen

Learning how to effectively respond to perfectionism is harder than giving in to it. We face constant pressure to excel; society respects us if we're successful and shames us for not being successful—by its standards. We've been conditioned to admire people who revolutionize industries, start media empires, paint masterpieces, and build life-changing apps. Often, when we hear about what these people had to give up to get to where they are, we only laud their passion and dedication even more. We look at Steve Jobs and marvel at his unparalleled success with Apple and Pixar, even romanticizing his perfectionism, which famously manifested as being harsh to his colleagues and employees when they didn't meet his standards and having barren rooms in his home because he couldn't find the right furniture. The message we're fed is: it's all worth it if you're successful.

Society gauges success in terms of accolades and material output, so, naturally, you want to be the person who wins the most awards, works at the organization with the biggest name, goes on the most extravagant vacations, lives in the fanciest neighborhood, or has the most expensive car. But by conceding to society's definition of *your* worth, you're measuring the goodness of your life with a yardstick that doesn't actually bring you fulfillment. This is the ever-present, inevitable trap of success. Thus, even when you make real changes and use the skills in this book, you'll still be pushed toward old unhelpful patterns by a culture that compels you to court success, regardless of the cost to your needs and well-being. Here's how to stay out of the game.

Practice, Practice, Practice

The temptation to play the game of perfectionism will show up again and again: you'll agree to help your parents with their yardwork when you haven't cleaned your own apartment in months; you'll deliberate on which Dutch oven to buy for way too long; you'll spend a crisp New England fall day editing a book chapter instead of going outside; and on and on. This is what you know to do: chase the elusive victory at whatever cost. Neither do our brilliant minds stop problem solving and rationalizing just because we've clarified our values. They still have their rules and unyielding expectations, worries and fears, what-ifs and abhorrent prophecies. That's what they know to do.

We've already talked about the skills, tips, and tricks to disrupt your mind's entrenched patterns. You now have the skeleton of progress. To add flesh to it, you need to practice, practice, practice—times infinity. It takes more than dismantling old patterns; you'll also need to build new adaptive ones and make them stick. Psychological skills are similar to all the other skills in our lives: sports, writing, dancing, talking to new people, cooking, and so forth. The difference is, you can practice psychological skills literally anywhere, because your thoughts and emotions are *always* present. You're constantly thinking and feeling. Even the observation that "my mind is blank right now" is a thought. In the perpetual presence of thoughts and feelings, you *always* have the choice of values over fear—whether or not it's obvious or feels possible in the moment.

So wherever and whenever you notice a nagging thought ("If only I had started two days earlier…"), anxiety rippling through your torso, or the drone of self-criticism ("I can never do anything right"), *practice*. Practice recognizing thoughts as thoughts and letting them float through your mind space—like a plastic bag in the wind. You might even appreciate that your mind is trying to help, even if it's doing a poor job. Practice stepping back from anxiety and observing its journey through your body, as if you were an astronomer studying the path of a rogue comet. Practice identifying self-labels and self-stories and reconnecting with your self (or nonself) from a dispassionate and curious vantage point, as though you were an anthropologist studying a new population. In all these scenarios, practice being in the here and now, gently welcoming thoughts and feelings as they flit through time and space. And at every possible juncture, practice pivoting toward your values.

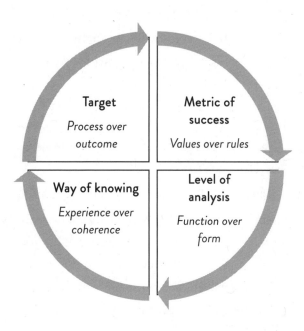

Aim to practice several times a day. Even twice a day starts to add up, as you'll be clocking fourteen practice sessions a week. Remember how psychological skills are similar to any other skill? Imagine practicing piano or German fourteen times a week. You'll get better at anything you do fourteen times every week. If your mind is going, "Great plan—once I have more time and energy, I'll commit to practicing at least twice a day," see if you can notice this thought as a thought, make room for the discomfort of committing to something you don't feel entirely prepared for, and go for it anyway. That's your first practice session for the day.

Continue to find opportunities throughout your week. Typically, we don't lack opportunities for practice as much as *awareness* of opportunities for practice. When you feel frustrated with your children for not packing their lunch, turn to your value of being a supportive parent and help them. When you feel trepidation around trying something new, choose your value of learning and take the risk of asking a "dumb" question. When you notice reluctance to leave for a road trip because your bags aren't packed exactly how you want them, choose your value of adventure and get on the open road. When you think about hiding your mediocre assignment from judgment, choose your value of self-improvement and ask for feedback anyway. There are countless examples. They're all around you—once you know to look for them.

The Perfectionism Menace

When you're well on your way to making changes in line with your values, you might notice a familiar presence. A little voice saying you can do *even more* for your values, innocently asking if you're sure you've chosen the right values. That's perfectionism again. People don't—and can't—*unlearn* behaviors, which means you don't forget behaviors even when you stop doing them, especially those that are well-worn and ingrained in your system. That's why you pick up things you've done before more easily the second time around, like riding a bike for the first time in years, and why you can still remember the phone number you had growing up or your first email address—the brain remembers.

How learning works is that you acquire new behaviors that become more accessible than old ones, such as staying quiet when a relative takes a controversial stance on a social issue *instead of* arguing. You *relearn* what to do in various situations, even when your original instinct to roll your eyes doesn't go away. Relatedly, you'll never completely eliminate the urge to do things perfectly. Instead, you'll form new patterns that loop over old ones, just as you'll get better at nodding along to keep the peace at family dinners the more you practice.

These new patterns may even look the same as old ones. Hence, relearning may entail doing the exact same behaviors as before but for new reasons, like exercising to boost your physical health rather than to hit a certain weight. By the same token, if you're meditating because mindfulness is one of your values and you feel like you *should*, that's a red flag. This is the same function of following a rule, just in a new form. The target of change is function, not form.

It's exceedingly easy to fall into the trap of trying to live out your values perfectly or following your values rigidly; in this case, you've replaced rules with "values." Rather than "I *should* be perfect," you now have "I *should* be consistent with my values." We enclose "values" in quotation marks because they end up functioning like rules. Treating values as the "correct" answer to your life equation puts you right back in the belly of perfectionism, and you'll feel just as anxious, stressed, and worried as you did pre-values.

Pay attention to when following your "values" feels like following rules. You may experience fear of failure, guilt, shame, urgency, or self-doubt. This emotional data tells you what's motivating your behaviors—and it's not values. If you catch perfectionism taking over values, you have a few options.

Check your values. Go back to the values drawing board. Perhaps the values you selected don't really make you content—that happens. You learn through doing and experiencing. For instance, if you identified volunteerism as a value and later realized that you derived no fulfillment whatsoever from washing blankets at the animal shelter, then maybe it isn't one of your values. Strike it off your list and focus on your other values. You can always add it back to your list if things change.

Check your actions. Alternatively, maybe your *actions* aren't aligned with your values. Let's say you chose to spend a weekend of quality time with your parents based on your value of family and regretted the decision. You felt stressed the entire time and didn't perceive the payoff to be worth the cost—even though family is unequivocally important to you. If so, your value of family might manifest differently from what you had originally articulated. In this case, *redefine* the value and brainstorm new actions to test out. For instance, you could instead check in with your parents once a week, spend more time with your children, or read a book about parenting to see if those actions match up more accurately. Then continue to refine your value of family based on the data you glean from these new experiences. You'll know if you're following your values because the quality of an activity is transformed when you realize the purpose behind it.

Connect with your values. When alignment between values and actions feels off, the other move is to consciously orient yourself toward your values. In this case, you know the value is meaningful and the action is in line with the value, yet there's a barrier keeping you from experiencing the value fully. For example, you could, in theory, sit through your fiftieth wedding anniversary celebration with your mind wholly preoccupied with the muddy guest shoes in your hallway, whether you've prepared enough food, and the cleanup you'll have to do afterward. By the end of the party, this milestone will have flown by and you'll have missed out on reminiscing over the decades you've spent with your partner: the diapers that needed changing, the quarrels over which shows to watch, the shared moments of silent understanding, the belly-aching laughs, the loss of mutual friends, and so much more. You wouldn't get to appreciate your spouse's speech about how wonderful you are and how they couldn't have asked for anything different. You know you care about all this. Unfortunately, you're disconnected from the values right in front of you. In other words, everything you need is there. All that's left is for you to recognize your values, link your values to your actions or vice versa, and get in touch with the part of you that cares deeply.

Create variability. Another way to undermine rigid rule following is to deliberately create variability. Given that humans are creatures of habit for the most part, it's challenging to naturally vary your behavior. That's why you fall into routines and have your set way of making coffee in the morning and cleaning (or not cleaning) your kitchen. It's also why you would likely struggle to pick up counterintuitive sports, like rock climbing and weight lifting, without explicit instruction (such as, use your toes, not your soles). Generally, people stick to what they know or what makes sense (that's the coherence trap) and don't vary their behaviors enough to chance upon more constructive moves.

To create variability, you need to actively try out new options. Your mind may assure you that it already knows what's going to happen when you do that and you're not going to like it. However, as much as your mind thinks it knows it all, you can't always know whether you like or dislike something unless you experience it for yourself. Opening yourself up to unfamiliar experiences, like when you let your children choose family activities, allows you to practice flexibility, learn things outside your comfort zone, and discover other values or new ways of enacting values. You may like the new activities or hate them, but the point is, you'll have created variability, and this variability can lead you to treasures you never knew you wanted.

Failure Is an Option

You can do *a lot* to stay on the path of your values, and the human in you is still going to falter. When that inevitably happens, sidestep the all-or-nothing calculus. The perfectionistic mind likes to put things in neat categories: good or bad, right or wrong, success or failure. It'll do the same thing when you get offtrack from your goals and values. "Oh, you weren't absolutely consistent with your values? Then you've failed." Your mind tells you to cut your losses, call it quits, and marinate in the shame of utter ineptitude. But that's like leaving yourself to the mountain lions once you veer off the designated hiking trail. Wouldn't it be wiser to find your way back to the trail and resume your hike? After all, the peak of the mountain doesn't vanish because you go off-trail. It's still there for you to ascend. Remember, the option to choose your values over your fears is *always* there for you.

At the same time, maybe check in with yourself before you plod on. Do you really want to get back on track? Perhaps this is perfectionism working in the other direction: "shoulding" you into finishing the hike you've already started. (This is why tracking the function of behaviors is vital; we can tell whether a behavior is helpful only when we know what it's about.) Perfectionism says there's no turning back now—even when your parked car is still in sight. However, maybe you don't really want to complete the hike, and you've locked yourself into a value you now believe you have to pursue—that's treating values as rules again.

Here's a controversial idea: failure *is* an option. At least, failure as perfectionism defines it. We mean knowing when to quit and following through. We tend to use "quitting" and "failing" synonymously when there's no basis for that. In fact, the etymology of "quit" is about being set free (from war, from debts, etc.), which seems applicable even today: when you quit, you free yourself from an obligation, usually one that's been arbitrarily imposed in the case of perfectionism.

So return to curiosity. *Why* are you hiking in the first place? What would quitting or completing the hike do for you? Pause, breathe, and notice the brewing storm on your mind's horizon: the urge to give up, the pressure to keep going, torrential fear and worry, the downpour of self-criticism. Simply watch the storm, knowing that it can't do anything to you. Create distance from the storm. Look to your values. Where do you want to be once the storm passes?

Following the Valued Brick Road

Changing habits is challenging, and there's no foolproof formula for it. The two of us have studied how to influence human behavior for literally decades, and we still can't guarantee anyone sustainable lifestyle changes.

In fact, we ourselves also persist in unhealthy habits despite our reading and researching: Clarissa struggles to leave unread emails alone, and Mike procrastinates busywork until he gets emails about it.

Let's be clear: you will fail at this. You'll mess up, *and* you'll find your way back to your values. Just like you'd find your way back to the interstate if you took a wrong exit instead of resigning yourself to a life in Kansas. Failing is part of growing as much as falling is part of learning how to walk. We learn from our missteps and get stronger each time we get back up again. Remember, the muscle you're building is *getting back on track*. Each time you reorient to your values and follow through on your commitments, you're progressing toward the person you want to be. If you're working on being more accepting of your flaws, for example, you may still find yourself spending hours editing and refining your work, ruminating on how awkward you were on your date, and admonishing yourself for mixing up meeting times. The urge to be the perfect version of yourself or to avoid failure won't go away. Part of the work is to ground yourself in your values, reminding yourself that you care about self-kindness and work–play balance, and to choose behaviors in line with what matters at the next opportunity.

Admittedly, the obstacles each of us faces are uneven. The oppressive structures baked into our culture and institutions make sure of that. Thus, some of us may find enacting change a matter of resolve, whereas others with marginalized identities have to navigate around obnoxious roadblocks every step of the way. These roadblocks are real. Identifying values and committing to action don't erase systemic barriers. The skills we've discussed help with pursuing things that matter when unpleasant thoughts and feelings tell us not to, but they don't solve injustice and inequity (at least not directly). This book may help you become a more loving and mindful parent, but it can't change access to affordable child care or give you the privilege to take time off work. Our realistic hope is that you'll be empowered to pursue your values even if you can't do it perfectly, even if it feels like stress and worry are weighing you down, and even if you fail in the process. That's it.

This is *your* life. It's yours to live or let slip away. We can't tell you what to do, because the only person you ultimately have to answer to is yourself. No one but you experiences your pain and joy, and no one but you can take responsibility for your actions and inactions. With every choice you make, you alter your trajectory, and over time, these seemingly inconsequential decisions make up the fabric of your life. What is the life you want to create for yourself?

* * *

Making progress toward your values is hard work. The work equates to practicing the skills in this book as much as possible to build your technique and strength—and then to maintain them going forward. Because our culture reinforces striving for success, perfectionistic tendencies (like avoiding mistakes, pleasing others, and self-criticizing) will return. In those instances, observe the tendencies without acting on them and implement appropriate strategies to keep yourself from reverting to old habits.

Nevertheless, even with all the mindfulness and effort, you will mess up; mistakes are unavoidable. Plus, anxiety, stress, and worry are always going to be lurking around. Rather than beat yourself up for failing to embrace imperfection, reorient to your values when you get off-track and resume your journey. At the end of the day, this is *your* life we're talking about. Go live it.

Acknowledgments

Clarissa: The people who have validated, reassured, commiserated with, and supported me in more ways than I can name: Nova, Megan, Gabe, Dhanna, and Danyel.

Eric for reminding me that some (most) things don't matter.

Sarah for your infinite patience, wisdom, and compassion.

Mike for always encouraging me to do more than my mind tells me I can.

Mike: Thanks to Jeff Szymanski at the International OCD Foundation and the anonymous donor who funded our work on clinical perfectionism.

All the participants who were in our studies.

Utah State University for supporting research.

My graduate students, who are always teaching me.

Clarissa, you'll always be my Kawhi Leonard.

References

Bieling, P. J., A. L. Israeli, and M. M. Antony. 2004. "Is Perfectionism Good, Bad, or Both? Examining Models of the Perfectionism Construct." *Personality and Individual Differences* 36(6): 1373–1385.

Egan, S. J., T. D. Wade, and R. Shafran. 2011. "Perfectionism as a Transdiagnostic Process: A Clinical Review." *Clinical Psychology Review* 31(2): 203–212.

Hayes, S. C., and B. T. Sanford. 2014. "Cooperation Came First: Evolution and Human Cognition." *Journal of the Experimental Analysis of Behavior* 101(1): 112–129.

Park, H., and D. Y. Jeong. 2015. "Psychological Well-Being, Life Satisfaction, and Self-Esteem Among Adaptive Perfectionists, Maladaptive Perfectionists, and Nonperfectionists." *Personality and Individual Differences* 72: 165–170.

Prud'homme, J., D. M. Dunkley, E. Bernier, J.-L. Berg, A. Ghelerter, and C. J. Starrs. 2017. "Specific Perfectionism Components Predicting Daily Stress, Coping, and Negative Affect Six Months and Three Years Later." *Personality and Individual Differences* 111: 134–138.

Stoeber, J., and L. E. Damian. 2014. "The Clinical Perfectionism Questionnaire: Further Evidence for Two Factors Capturing Perfectionistic Strivings and Concerns." *Personality and Individual Differences* 61–62: 38–42.

Stoeber, J., and K. Otto. 2006. "Positive Conceptions of Perfectionism: Approaches, Evidence, Challenges." *Personality and Social Psychology Review* 10(4): 295–319.

Suh, H., P. B. Gnilka, and K. G. Rice. 2017. "Perfectionism and Well-Being: A Positive Psychology Framework." *Personality and Individual Differences* 111: 25–30.

Clarissa W. Ong, PhD, is a postdoctoral associate at the Center for Anxiety and Related Disorders at Boston University. She received her doctoral degree in clinical/counseling psychology from Utah State University, and completed her clinical internship at McLean Hospital/Harvard Medical School. Her research interests include acceptance and commitment therapy (ACT), process-based therapy, obsessive-compulsive disorder (OCD), hoarding disorder, and perfectionism. She has contributed to more than sixty peer-reviewed publications and a book. She has also received funding from the Association for Contextual Behavioral Science (ACBS).

Michael P. Twohig, PhD, is well known for his work in ACT and OCD, which is closely related to perfectionism. Twohig is professor in the psychology department at Utah State University. He is past president of the ACBS, and a current member of the Association for Behavioral and Cognitive Therapies (ABCT). He has written more than 170 peer-reviewed publications, seven books, and has received funding from many organizations, including the National Institute of Mental Health (NIMH).

Foreword writer **Randy O. Frost, PhD**, teaches abnormal psychology at Smith College in Northampton, MA. He is coauthor of *Buried in Treasures*.

MORE BOOKS from
NEW HARBINGER PUBLICATIONS

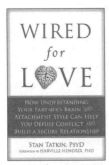
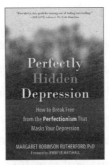

Real change *is* possible

For more than forty-five years, New Harbinger has published proven-effective self-help books and pioneering workbooks to help readers of all ages and backgrounds improve mental health and well-being, and achieve lasting personal growth. In addition, our spirituality books offer profound guidance for deepening awareness and cultivating healing, self-discovery, and fulfillment.

Founded by psychologist Matthew McKay and Patrick Fanning, New Harbinger is proud to be an independent, employee-owned company. Our books reflect our core values of integrity, innovation, commitment, sustainability, compassion, and trust. Written by leaders in the field and recommended by therapists worldwide, New Harbinger books are practical, accessible, and provide real tools for real change.

 **newharbinger**publications